Praise for the book, '*Success at School* and *Beyond*'

"I have just finished reading Enza's book. It is one of the most informative, balanced books I have read on building self confidence in your child. I really do wish I had something like this when I was raising my own children. I think I raised them on a wing and a prayer. I am now a grandmother and find it one of my deepest joys to be fully involved in my grandchildren's lives. I have learnt a lot from Enza's book, which I plan to put into practice – I plan to 'Be in the Moment' much more – it is so easy to be busy doing something and miss opportunities for fun. Thank you, Enza, for this timely reminder. I wish you every success with your book and your future endeavours in this most important field."

Judy, mother and grandmother

"Thank you, Enza. I read your book, then I read it again and again. Each time I learnt something to help me as a new mum, and to give my boy the best start to life. It's great to refresh what is essentially important to guiding my child to a happy, fulfilling life. Thank you for all the great ideas. I'm excited to put those ideas into practice."

Lisa, mother

"What a wonderful book, written from the heart, and filled with gems of wisdom and information. It reflects the many years of personal research and education Enza has devoted to child growth and development, motivated by her deep desire to see every child has the best opportunity for happiness and to reach their full potential. It also reflects the wisdom of her own experiences as a mother and grandmother.

Some time ago, when my children were young, I had the opportunity to attend a workshop on Brain Gym® that Enza conducted. Brain Gym® became an integral part of my daughter's daily routine with obvious and very positive results. It does work, and so do the many other insightful and valuable principles and techniques Enza has shared in this book. I now have two healthy, happy, and successful adult daughters. Enza, I applaud your passion, dedication, and desire to share the valuable knowledge and wisdom you have acquired over the years, and highly recommend this book to every parent and parent to be."

Debbie, mother

"When I was a university student in Brisbane, Enza helped me to find balance in my life and to gain a greater awareness of how stress negatively impacts the body and mental functioning. Conversely, I also learned how the right nutrition, positive thoughts, and simple exercises can help to heal the body. Many of the concepts that Enza taught me have stayed with me even today and influenced my understanding of the important connections between the body and mind. It is with great pleasure that I have read this book and have been reminded of these important concepts again. Now, as a young mother, I look forward to applying these techniques and principles in raising my own daughter in a positive and loving environment and to see her grow up to be a confident, happy, and capable young girl."

Michelle, mother and business owner

Success at School and Beyond

7 simple steps to boost your child's ability to learn, confidence and self-esteem for greater success at school and in life

'Having fun and being in the moment developing a happier, healthier and confident child'

by Enza Lyons

Parent Guide
Success at School and Beyond
7 simple steps to boost your child's ability to learn,
confidence and self-esteem for greater success at school
and in life by Enza Lyons

Enza Lyons
P.O. Box 205,
Mt Ommaney Qld 4074 Australia
Website: www.dlhc.com.au
Published by Enza Lyons
Brisbane, Queensland, Australia
Cover designed by Ngirl Design

Catalogue-in-Publications details available on request from the Australian
National Library

ISBN: 978-0-9873415-2-5 (pbk)

Also available as an ebook: 978-0-9873415-3-2 (ebk)

Medical Disclaimer

The information contained herein is not intended to diagnose, treat, cure
or prevent any disease, nor should it be used as a substitute for your own
physician's advice. The author recommends that you do your own research
and consult a qualified medical health professional before choosing to
pursue a medical treatment plan. Before beginning any exercise program,
it is advisable to check with your professional healthcare practitioner. The
information is for educational purposes only in believing that readers will
become more informed on the choices that are available. I encourage you to
become an educated person because ultimately the choices made, are up to
you and that you take full responsibility for your decisions. Every effort has
been made to ensure that the information presented in this book is accurate.

Brain Gym® is a registered trademark of Brain Gym® International/Educational
Kinesiology Foundation

Table of Contents

Acknowledgements i

About the Author – My personal journey. iii

Introduction ix

Chapter 1   Step # 1 - Being a playful parent. 1

Chapter 2   Step # 2 - Recognise that your child is unique 17

Chapter 3   Step # 3 - Give them what they need to grow. 33

Chapter 4   Step # 4 - Empower your child to be their best selves 58

Chapter 5   Step # 5 - Give your child the skills to succeed in life 82

Chapter 6   Step # 6 - Use music to enhance learning and confidence. 99

Chapter 7   Step # 7 - Reduce stress and empower your child to become

             calmer, happier and successful. 106

Chapter 8   Conclusion. 119

Chapter 9   Finding Support 126

Acknowledgements

Thank you, especially to my family, who have really made a great difference in my life. To my husband and closest friend, Keith, for his unending support, encouragement, and love. To my parents and my extended family, who have given me love and support.

I like to dedicate this book to my children and grandchildren, who are the joy and fun of my life. They all have enriched my life and taught me so much about unconditional love and given me the life experience to grow, develop, mature, and appreciate life to be a content, patient, thankful, forgiving, loving and happier person.

Thank you to the numerous researchers, educators, and therapists whose work has contributed enormously to my life and my work. Thank you to my friends and many others who have supported me.

Thank you to my clients, who have taught me so much and have allowed me to share their success stories.

Learning about the joys of raising the next generation is a privilege and a blessing. Being a parent and grandparent is both challenging and rewarding, frustrating and joyous. Building a relationship with a child is a never-ending process. It is the most fulfilling job a person can do. Children are wonderful gifts, a blessing from God.

About the Author — My personal journey

Hello and welcome. I'm Enza Lyons and I want to share with you *Success at School and Beyond,* seven simple steps to boost your child's ability to learn, to have more confidence and self-esteem, for greater success in school and in life.

Being a parent has its good days and bad days. On those good days parenting can be a breeze and you have lovely perfect children behaving well, and you are feeling good connecting with your children. On those bad days, parenting can be confusing, frustrating and challenging. Being a parent can feel lonely at times. You may feel that you are being judged for everything you do especially when your child is having a temper tantrum in the shopping centre or misbehaving in the classroom. You may wonder what type of parent you are, feeling guilty for some of your mistakes or wondering why your child is doing what he or she is doing. Your child may misbehave, be intense, noisy, persistent, strong-willed, ultra-sensitive, easily display temper tantrums, moody, unable to adapt to new situations, fearful, anxious or energetic. You may feel you have had enough. I felt like this many times as many mothers do when they get tired and stressed from their busy family life. I searched for books to get encouragement from others, to seek for spiritual strength and broaden my mind, to learn better ways to manage my children and to guide my life to move forward.

I have learnt that while I was teaching my children all about life, they taught me what 'Life' was all about. I am still on that journey as I have grandchildren. I trust that you may find some helpful tips in this book that will help you and your child work through the issues you are having and set them on the path to social and academic success. I have written this book to make it easier for you. The wise owl symbol at the end of each chapter is the spot for you to write an action plan, to write the ideas, tips and activities you would like to implement for you and your family.

For over 23 years in my private practice, I have worked with children and adults using a simple yet powerful system. You can dramatically improve your family's physical, emotional, and mental well-being. It's about a healthy mind, healthy body, and healthy living. I have assisted many struggling with concentration, reading, writing, math, and with early learning difficulties, including ADD, ADHD, dyspraxia, autism, dyslexia, trauma, delayed development, anxiety, depression, injuries and other challenges. The results have been amazing using safe, unconventional educational programs and natural therapies such as Kinesiology, Brain Gym® and Rhythmic Movement Training to transform my client's lives.

It is for these reasons that I am so delighted to introduce to you these simple, yet powerful techniques and gems of information which have helped thousands of children to achieve their full potential for learning – children just like yours!

My interest in natural therapies to achieve optimal health and performance began earlier in life. At the age of 18, I was experiencing a number of health problems, including severe acne. After studying everything I could on nutrition, exercise, and other natural health principles, I was able to implement a program that cleared my acne, radically improved my general health, and boosted my energy.

Years later I was married, and after the birth of my second child, I began suffering from lingering lower back pain. After receiving only temporary relief from chiropractic treatment, I visited a Kinesiology practitioner and was astonished by the immediate results. I wanted to know more about this amazing science.

Life was busy managing a family business and raising two children. Then I began to receive letters from the school. My son was having difficulties in his first grade – struggling with completing his work and disrupting class to the extent that he was sent out to the hallway. I could not ignore it. He was anxious and defeated. He did not want to go to school anymore. He was 'assessed', but no one was able to offer any practical advice in those days. I was upset, anxious and feeling helpless. I couldn't understand why such a bright child was having these problems.

So began my journey to learn everything I could about the brain, child development, nutrition, and health. I researched and read hundreds of books over the years, looking for answers to my questions. I was motivated to learn how to help my family to be happier, healthier, and more successful in life.

Fortunately, I discovered Kinesiology and Brain Gym®. At the time, I was very excited to discover these safe and natural ways to help my son, yet at that time his teachers weren't interested. Now, thousands of teachers and parents, in over 80 countries, sing praises for Brain Gym® because of the transformational improvements in their students in the classroom. Children are happier, achieve better grades, gain calm confidence, and perform better in sports and music. Adults improve concentration and memory, conquer fears and anxiety, and achieve balance and a sense of well-being.

In the integrative health field, Kinesiology uses movement and muscle testing to detect and release imbalances or stresses in the body. Brain Gym® is part of Educational Kinesiology – an educational program set up by Dr Paul Dennison Phd., using movement to increase the physical skills of daily life activities, promoting the joy of learning for more efficient learning and quality of life. Attending the workshops helped me to understand how I could assist my children. I also learnt how to reduce my own anxiety and stress levels, at the same time improving my learning and organisational skills. I learnt skills to re-wire the brain, changing old habits and patterns of thinking to new, positive patterns.

Many think that Brain Gym® is only for children, to help them develop all kinds of academic, coordination, and interpersonal skills. Now, the secret is out, and adults are using Brain Gym® movements to help themselves! Workers are more focused and productive in the workplace. Athletes and musicians are better coordinated and mentally ready to perform at their peak. Parents are able to reduce stress levels, improve their child's behaviour, and bring harmony into the home.

Over thirty years ago, I began this journey where these programs assisted me, my family, and friends. Since then, I have worked with thousands of clients.

Now, as a grandmother, I look back at my life's experiences, mistakes, successes, and positive lessons that have formed my perception about raising children. Many emotions are triggered and released; often, I wish I could change some of these mistakes for the better. Most parents and grandparents will relate to this. Some things I could not change no matter what I did, so I moved forward in other ways. I've made mistakes. I've had successes. Raising a happy, healthy, and well-adjusted child is challenging, especially in the fast-paced world that we live in today. Your attitude towards this all-important job is what will make it fun and exciting for both of you. I encourage you to have a love for learning and be continuously open to new understanding. Forgiveness, love and thankfulness have a way of releasing challenging emotions and memories.

We are all learners. Our life is a growing and maturing process, just like a rose plant growing from a cutting. The plant has to be watered, as it lives, in highly nourishing soil, receiving sunshine, being treated gently, producing beautiful roses and being admired. So it is for our children. We are to nurture our children, giving them the nourishment they need to grow, guiding, teaching, disciplining, loving and admiring them. Life's experiences and pressures will shape them to grow to become who they are.

We are living in a fast-changing world and the way we do things during our child's first twelve years of life will form the basis for their future successes. Life is busy, years fly by, and before you realise it, your children will be teenagers. Becoming more informed and finding positive, effective strategies and techniques to use for your child early in life can completely turn things around for them. I trust you can learn from my experiences. You may like to adopt into your life some of the knowledge and wisdom I have gained through my life's experiences.

A parent's dream is to see their children grow up to be happy, healthy, confident and successful in life.

This book is a step towards a better life for you, your child, and everyone around you! I encourage you to be open and curious, and enjoy exploring new information that you can add in your journey of life.

I wish you and your family vibrant health, mental clarity, and radiant well-being. You deserve it!

Enza Lyons
Licensed Brain Gym® Teacher/Consultant (Brain Gym®
International/Edu-K Foundation)
Kinesiology Practitioner (Member of A.K.A., A.T.M.S.)
Learning & Behavioural Specialist
Rhythmic Movement Training Consultant
Workplace Performance Coach
www.dlhc.com.au

INTRODUCTION

Children learn what they live

If a child lives with criticism, he learns to condemn.
If a child lives with hostility, he learns to fight.
If a child lives with fear, he learns to be apprehensive.
If a child lives with pity, he learns to feel sorry for himself.
If a child lives with ridicule, he learns to be shy.
If a child lives with jealousy, he learns what envy is.
If a child lives with shame, he learns to feel guilty.
If a child lives with encouragement, he learns to be confident.
If a child lives with tolerance, he learns to be patient.
If a child lives with praise, he learns to be appreciative.
If a child lives with acceptance, he learns to love.
If a child lives with approval, he learns to like himself.
If a child lives with recognition, he learns that it is good to have a goal.
If a child lives with sharing, he learns about generosity.
If a child lives with honesty and fairness, he learns what truth and justice are.
If a child lives with friendliness, he learns that the world is a nice place in which to live.
If you live with serenity, your child will live with peace of mind.
With what is your child living?

Dorothy Law Nolte

When I first read this poem, it made me stop and think about what I was doing as a parent. It was a positive change for me to be aware that our children learned by our example in every way. Once you become aware of your influence on your child as they watch your every action, you can consciously work on changing and reprogramming your inappropriate behaviour to a new and positive way.

Honouring your child's gifts

Self-esteem is vital for everyone, and is deeply affected by the values parents place on the child's gifts, abilities, and efforts.

A child is born with potential, like a seedling.

All that a child can become is the result of four things:

1. Potential

2. Education

3. Opportunity

4. Effort

What determines the difference between one child and the next is simply how they are trained, educated, and guided.

Dr. Bruce Lipton Ph.D., author of Biology of Belief says, *"Your children's genes reflect only their potential, not their destiny. It is up to you to provide the environment that allows them to develop to their highest potential.*

No one can be a perfect parent, yet there are many ways to be a caring, positive and loving parent. It all begins with a loving attitude to this all important task.

Each of us take on many different roles in life – we are sons and daughters, spouses, employees, club members, friends, writers, teachers, and much more. I believe that no role in the world is as important as that of being a parent. As a parent, you are responsible for equipping a young person to be happy, healthy, confident, responsible and successful in this world.

Here then, are some of the ideas I will expand upon within this book—ideas that will bring you and your child more peace, less stress, and a happy and balanced life. This is the opportunity for you to be open, intuitive, and confident to adopt whatever works for you and your family by *having fun and being in the moment.*

Have a plan

Children, unlike automobiles, television sets, and even puppies, do not come with owner's manuals – and there are no mandatory parenting classes. It all adds up to lots of trial and error, and figuring out for ourselves what works for our lives, our families, and our children. That is where this book comes in! Rather than just "winging it", I would like to give you ideas, research, tips, and steps for raising happy, healthy, well-rounded children.

Where is the love?

Parenting with passion and purpose that results in raising happy and emotionally intelligent children, could be one of every parent's life goals. When your children know how much you love them, they will do their best to please you, making it easier to share happy and fulfilling lives together.

Be there in the moment and offer praise when they succeed.

"Well done sweetheart. You did something new. You must feel happy." Take the time to tell them how amazing they are and help them to become aware of their personal talents and interests. Your positive words and actions will support them to do the things they love moving towards their purpose in life. As children are growing up they are curious seeking answers to profound questions and set out to solve challenging issues in their lives. This is the opportunity to be a constant source of love, support and guidance.

Beliefs and values

Parents have an overwhelming influence on their children up to the age of 12. It is important during their formative years to teach them what they need to know about life. It is vital they know what you believe and understand your value system for their safety and well-being. As your child grows and develops, these beliefs will guide them throughout their life.

> *"Children are likely to live up to what you believe of them."*
> Lady Bird Johnson

Being a great example

Children watch, and record mentally, everything they see you say or do because they love you. They will follow your lead, whether good or bad; often, they will say what you say, act the way you act, and believe what you believe.

If your children see you model positive self-esteem, they will learn to do the same. I encourage you to be a good listener, so they will be too. Be respectful, patient, kind, encouraging, honest, truthful, and thankful. Keep the door to communication always open. Children learn far more from us than we ever intend to teach. *Be aware and be in the moment.*

The test of a good parent is to ask yourself a simple question: Would you be happy if your children grew up to be like you? If not, it is never too late to start learning and teaching good habits!

Community has an impact

I have learned that the community has an impact on the child. As a parent, you are only one of the many influences in your child's life. Grandparents, relatives, siblings, teachers, neighbours, life experiences and the world, all play a part in influencing your child. When parents choose to see their child as a unique, curious, spirited, creative, energetic, lovely human being, it pulls the parent's focus to the child's strengths. As a parent, you can support your children to grow in a positive encouraging environment to become more accomplished in their life. As a guardian, you can do your best to protect your child from any physical, mental and emotional harm. Be aware, there are those in the community who wish to do harm to the innocent. It is important to teach your child how to make wise, safe and better choices for their own safety and wellbeing throughout their life.

Parents have impact on emotional well-being

By example show your children to be grateful for what they have, whether it is little or abundance. Children living in abundance may not fully appreciate the blessings they have. Being grateful puts their focus on the positive things in their lives. For those things that we focus our energy on, we draw more of it into our lives.

Additionally, children are typically happy when they see you being happy. You can choose to be happy as well, and the benefits of counting your blessings can make that happen. Dr Bruce H. Lipton, Ph.D., in his book, *The Biology of Belief*, speaks about what a great impact parents have on the emotional well-being of children and how that impact is the foundation of all success and failure. Know that you have the power to choose to be happy.

Common Conflicts

The most common conflicts in homes everywhere have to do with everyday situations. Situations like bedtimes and rising times, sharing toys and household chores, when to go out in the morning, when to come home at night, or what to buy at the store. If we fear that our needs are not met, we can be quickly led to anger, defensiveness, or aggression. Every member of the family trusts that their needs will be met. By addressing the person's needs, you can avert conflict. Welcome differences as problems to solve and opportunities to deepen family connections.

Lists and goals

Talk to the happiest and most well-rounded people you know and they will mention their goals and their to-do lists. Why do you think this is? Those to-do lists help them focus on what they want, and what they need to do to get what they want. Just think of the sense of accomplishment they have when they are able to cross off one of their goals after reaching it. I encourage you to make your own list of goals, and regularly check them off once they are achieved. Amplify the good by involving your children in your goals, by letting them see your list and see you checking them off – and best of all – having them create their own list of goals along with you.

Teaching children to set SMART goals will build character, confidence, and self-esteem. SMART goals are Specific Measurable Attainable Realistic Timely. When you make a list of your children's goals with them, help them also to make a task list of things they can do to reach their goals. When they complete a task, have a small celebration, such as giving them a high five or a special treat. Reaching a goal calls for something a little bigger, perhaps seeing a movie with Mum or Dad, getting the CD, movie, or book they have wanted, or earning a special privilege.

Develop a growth mindset

Practice small changes and these will add up to big differences:

➢ Be the best you can be

➢ Work and achieve

➢ It's okay to make mistakes – that is how we learn

➢ Make changes – ask yourself how you can improve next time

➢ Be grateful for everything

➢ Use exercises and techniques to handle emotions

➢ Choose not to be a victim of any situation

➢ Create your goals using visualisation; take action

➢ Know you can create happiness, good health, well-being and abundance

---

What are your immediate and long-term goals for your child?

➤ Do you want your child to trust you?

➤ Do you want your child to be independent or dependent?

➤ Do you want your child to be cooperative?

➤ Do you want your child to have an attitude of gratitude?

➤ Do you want your child to have a positive attitude?

➤ Do you want your child to be respectful?

➤ Do you want your child to openly communicate with you?

➤ Do you want your child to love themselves and love life?

➤ Do you want your child to go through life fulfilled and passionate?

➤ Do you want your child to have a sense of personal responsibility?

➤ Do you want your child to have the courage to live out their dreams?

'The reason so many individuals fail to achieve their goals in life is that they never really set them in the first place'

Dennis Waitley

Remember the law of attraction. *Ask, seek and receive.* What do you want in life? Connect and search in your heart and mind to find the answers. Be yourself. Believe in yourself. Honour yourself to be what you want. What does success look like to you? Picture what you want for yourself and your family. Where will you be in 7 years time? Commit to your dreams.

Here are some examples of headings for your list of goals. Look at the different areas you and your family can plan for a happier and successful future together. Start today!

Be clear and set your goals for

> ➢ health and fitness

> ➢ relationship building and activities with the family and the world around you

> ➢ education developing skills and talents - a love of reading and learning, music, dance, science and sports

> ➢ developing skills in earning income to achieve what you want in life

> ➢ career

> ➢ spiritual gifts such as being forgiving, grateful, kind, patient, joyful, at peace and serving others

You may like to set your list of goals for short and long term such as daily, every 30 days, yearly and every 7 years. Be specific.

Find your motivation. What does it mean to you? Take the time and create your dreams to a reality. The time is now. Act on it now. Opportunities will come and you have the choice to take action.

Know why you want it. You are the composer of your life and your family. It will be the legacy you leave for your children and others. Share your great gifts. Teach your child to do the same.

Go to Page 123 to set your goals.

By determining the outcome of your goals for your child, you will be able to work out your approach to your parenting journey to get your desired results. Otherwise, you experience anxiety, frustration, and stress. It is no different to baking a cake, and then leaving out the eggs and adding too much salt and not enough flour. Too much of one ingredient and not enough of another can affect the outcome. You will not get the delicious cake you wanted. By identifying the intended outcome, then applying the proper ingredients to achieve the desired results you wanted, you will achieve joy and a successful outcome.

You can do your best to plan your future yet sometimes it does not always work out the way you would have liked it. There are days that test you. Through challenges you will grow. So often we focus on obstacles instead of focusing on what you want to achieve for yourself and your child. It is all about choice. Choose the habits that lead to success. Learn from successful people.

Challenges for parents and teachers

The major challenge for teachers and parents is to recognise the unique ability of how every child learns. We will cover how to recognise your child's unique learning style in depth in Chapter two. By evaluating the student's learning styles, and then creating strategies that work with how they learn best, learning becomes fun and easier. Teachers can guide their students to learn well and teach them the way they can learn effectively. Only then can they learn confidently and successfully.

To 'educate' means to draw forth

Parent-educators need to be sensitive to the child's natural abilities, gifts, and readiness to learn as these unfold. The parent is there both to support and to challenge. It is also essential to learn what challenges exist for children in the outside world. If there are drugs at school, teach them how to deal with the drugs. If all their friends watch TV, then educate and guide them about TV. If you do not know the answer to a problem, then research it and find the best answer that suits you and your child. There is wisdom in asking advice from professionals, family, friends, and people walking the same path as you. You can make better choices when you get advice from several people you can trust.

 Write your action plan ideas here.

CHAPTER 1

Step # 1: Being a playful parent

If I had my child to raise over again

If I had my child to raise all over again,
I'd finger paint more, and point the finger less.
I'd do less correcting, and more connecting.
I'd take my eyes off my watch, and watch with my eyes.
I would care to know less, and know to care more.
I'd take more hikes and fly more kites.
I'd stop playing serious, and seriously play.
I'd run through more fields, and gaze at more stars.
I'd do more hugging, and less tugging.
I would be firm less often, and affirm much more.
I'd build self-esteem first, and the house later.
I'd teach less about the love of power, and more about the power of love.
  Dianne Loomans, in the highly recommended *'Full Esteem Ahead'*

The daily life of a parent is filled with activities of getting the children ready for school, driving them to sports or music lessons and social events. Many parents express how there is little time to talk about the things that matter and just have fun together. Place a priority on putting aside time to do simple things and get in the habit of enjoying each other by playing games, singing, dancing, drawing, taking walks to the park, talking about hopes and dreams, snuggling, and hugging each other.

Playing with your children, and being playful overall, helps to nurture close connections with your child, encourage confidence, and solve some behaviour problems. It is important that children have good connections with their parents and their grandparents. Of course, parents are often busy with daily responsibilities and tired at the end of their long days.

Grandparents have the ability to play with their grandchildren to a much greater extent than parents, and that is probably one of the reasons why children are so close to their grandparents. As a grandparent, I fully appreciate how important play is for a child. Focus on having fun together, giggling, and connecting. It helps form a solid bond between you and them. Learn to awaken your family's creativity.

Michael Mendizza and Joseph Chilton Pearce's inspiring book *Magical Parent-Magical Child* makes it clear that play not programming is the key to optimizing the learning and performance of infants and children. Children need parents who can playfully foster the curiosity, creativity and wonder that accompanies their children into the world.

Playful parents

Infants gaze up at their mother and father with deep depths of love in their eyes, toddlers will grab you and hug you tight, and older children love to spend time with you reading or going for walks. It is these moments that you have to touch your child's (and your own) heartstrings; they form solid heart-to-heart connections and are the reward for all our diligent parenting.

Yes, there will be times when the baby is inconsolable, or your toddler throws himself on the floor because he cannot have the latest toy, your children fight with each other, or bury themselves in electronic escape devices. Being a playful parent can build a better bond with your child and encourage them to behave to please you.

Play brings deep emotional bonds; your children are happy, cooperative, creative, and engaged. What could possibly be a better time to interact with them?

Playtime is also when children explore and make sense of all the new experiences they have had, or recover from anything that has upset them. Sounds like they are on to something, doesn't it?

Play is harder for adults to do, because we have forgotten how to do it. With all the stress and obligations our daily lives demand of us, we really do not have much room in our lives for play. In fact, we might get tired or bored easily when playing with our children. To adults, playtime means leisure. For children, playing is their job.

In fact, playtime is quality time, a special time when children open up to their parents revealing what they are thinking. It is also a time to teach and guide them.

Playtime is fun time

A simple game like catch, with a parent and child tossing a ball back and forth, helps a child in numerous ways, such as hand-eye coordination, gross motor skills, self-confidence, and establishing a deeper connection between the two of you. Discovering the world and all they are able to do helps them develop confidence and self-esteem. Play fulfils the need for affection, closeness, and attachment, and helps them recover from emotional distress.

Have fun when you spend time with your children (and grandchildren). Sing silly songs, have pillow fights, tell jokes and stories, play peek-a-boo, tag, hide and seek, board games, or kickball. It does not really matter what sort of play it is; what matters is that you interact playfully with them and connect deeply. You can do this while making beds, playing sports, working on homework assignments, watching a movie, or just hanging out. It's all WORTH IT!

Why less TV really does mean better grades

Most parents and educators instinctively know that kids do better, in school and in life, if they spend less time 'vegging out' in front of the TV and more time playing, being outside, and interacting with others.

But why is that the case?

How do we learn?

The best place to start is by understanding how we learn.

Neuroscience has shown that from infancy the development of the brain relies on interaction with the surrounding environment through our senses and through movement.

Each interaction, each new movement and experience, activates new neural connections in our brain. The targeted movements of Brain

Gym® and Rhythmic Movements have been created to aid in this activation. As we stimulate and grow our brain in this way, we train our brain to think and learn better. Play is the most effective way of learning.

The power of play

Play comes naturally to children and, in fact, to the young of all mammals. Why? Because play engages all our senses and sparks a whole range of new movements – it develops the brain and the body.

This has been shown in the laboratory where rats and mice with the most enriched environments including room for movement and companions for play, display the most nerve cell growth – even in older rats and mice.

Embrace new ways to relax, play, and grow together. Use your imagination, colouring pencils, crayons and paint supplies, household objects, and enjoy being creative. Express and nurture family connections by doing creative activities together.

How does TV compare to play?

Obviously, sitting in front of the TV provides little interaction and movement. But worse than that, TV activates a stress response that can negatively impact learning.

Our natural survival response makes us acutely aware of danger signals, like the sudden changes in light that happen when we are watching TV, and these danger signals set off our stress response to prepare us for 'fight or flight'. But we can't fight the TV, and the flickering light makes it difficult to look away. So, we freeze. Within a short time, we go into a trance - being programmed by the TV. That's why advertisers use suggestive advertisements to sell their products to their audience.

Most parents would recognise this 'brain fog' or hypnotic state from when they have tried to talk with their children while the TV is on! And this doesn't even take into account the stressful content, like violence, that many children are exposed to through TV.

When we are in this stressed response state, our learning, memory, concentration, and reasoning are all affected.

Could TV be affecting your child's learning and development?

Is TV playing a big role in your child's life? TV has its good side. It can be entertaining and educational and can open up new worlds for children, giving them a chance to travel the globe, learn about different cultures, and new lifestyles. TV's negative side is that children are likely to learn things from it that parents do not want them to learn. TV can affect your child's health, sleep patterns, behaviour, and family life.

It is worthwhile to think about what role you want TV to play in your family life. Most children are now watching at least 4 ½ hours of television a day even as young as 4 months old. These children are more likely to have attention and behaviour problems by age 7, according to Dr Dimitri Christakes, professor of Paediatrics. Substantial research indicates that for children aged 2 years and younger, there can be adverse cognitive, behavioural, and physical health effects associated with television watching. The Canadian Paediatric Society and American Academy of Paediatrics discourage the use of television and other media for children under the age of 2, and recommend that after the age of 2, limiting both time and content of television programs watched by children.

Watch the YouTube video, *TEDx talk,* in which **Dr Dimitri Christakis, professor of Paediatrics** (whose research is quoted here), summarises current research on how television and other screen media affect young children's developing brain – with lifelong consequences.

➢ Early television viewing is related to later attention and behaviour problems. TV watching at the age of 1-3 years is associated with greater hyperactivity and attentional problems at the age of 7 years (Christakis et al., 2004). Efforts to limit television viewing in early childhood may be warranted, and there is more research being done.

➢ Different types of shows may have different effects on pre-schoolers' social competence and behaviour. For example, watching TV shows which promote pro-social behaviour, such as empathy and cooperation, is associated with better social competence and behaviour than watching TV shows which promote aggression and violence (Christakis et al., 2013).

It seems as a result of this research that the **best approach** is to limit the time children are in front of the screen. Carefully examine the shows your children watch and check how the television program promotes thinking, language development, and pro-social behaviour. Teach your children why not to watch the shows that encourage violence and inappropriate behaviour.

Research has shown that when parents spend more time with their children in their early years, reading books and doing playful activities, there is a better opportunity to increase their child's attention and improve their readiness to learn at school.

The recipe for reading success with your child is to be an enthusiastic parent, have several captivating books and a snugly comfortable nook. With lots of love allow plenty of time, enjoy heaps of laughter and have fun!

Today, there is such an increase in all sorts of technology for children. It is not only the television screen. There are computers, iPads and iPhones, and other electronic game systems where children spend hours playing games, and some of the games are violent. Many children are experiencing eye tension due to being in front of the screens for long hours. This eye tension causes ocular lock and children have difficulty smoothly eye-tracking across the page, which affects their reading ability.

Brain Gym® offers simple exercises with eye-tracking which releases tension in the eye muscles. Many of my students have improved their eye-tracking and reading within a month of doing the Brain Gym® exercises every day.

With all the technological advances, children are not getting the physical exercise and stimulation they require for normal development. It has become commonplace for children and adults to be diagnosed with ADD, ADHD and many other different labels, and then medicated. The side effects of these medications, such as Ritalin, are decreased appetite, insomnia, headaches, nervousness, stomach aches, heart palpitations, and even death. I urge you to be open, explore, and research different alternative solutions to assist your child naturally, such as Brain Gym and Rhythmic Movement.

The following is a testimonial from a happy mother who came to me seeking assistance to help her daughter.

"Our daughter was very volatile, easily distracted and moody. Her behaviour was so erratic that we spent months working with a child psychologist. While she was well behaved at school, her grades were low, she was easily distracted and had poor concentration.

We first heard about Enza's work through a friend. After Tayla's first session, we noticed an immediate change in her behaviour. Following two sessions of Brain Gym® Movement Training with Enza, Tayla's a totally different girl, she is more confident, less critical of herself and such a delightful little girl.

What an amazing transformation! I highly recommend Enza's services.
Janice, HR Manager, Mother

Less TV and more play equals better learning

There is a growing trend around the world to incorporate more free-flowing outdoor play in early education and minimise the time children spend in front of the TV.

Beginning in the 1950s in Denmark, forest kindergartens were developed to encourage children to explore, experiment, and learn through group play in a forest or natural environment. These forest kindergartens are now located across Europe, and recently, in the United States.

The underlying principle is that natural surroundings and human interaction stimulate learning. So start early with your child –

switch off the TV and take them outside for active play – and build a strong foundation for better learning and better grades.

Enjoying the natural beauty of the world

You may experience a sense of joy and calmness when you spend time admiring the natural beauty of the world around us, seeing the plants, flowers and trees, the clouds, stars and the universe, the beach and oceans, and all creatures great and small. So many times we find ourselves too busy to go outdoors and breathe in the fresh air and the view outdoors. It only takes a few minutes to go outside to visit your garden and smell the beautiful flowers, walk barefoot on the grass or listen to the sounds of birds singing.

When you place value and get excited about the beauty of nature around you, your children learn to share what they see around them. *'Wow! That's a beautiful flower.'*

Children are being educated to protect the environment, but without understanding how it truly came about, and experiencing the wonder of it. The passion is not really there.

27 ways to enjoy and value the natural beauty, harmony, and serenity our natural environment brings

1. Enjoy a nature walk in the park

2. Run on the grass barefoot

3. Feel the bark of different trees

4. Watch the clouds and how they form

5. Walk on the beach and collect shells

6. Visit a farm

7. Watch a sunset

8. Visit a flower show

9. Look for a bird nest

10. Look and find what birds are in your garden

11. Write names of the family in sand

12. Gaze at the stars at night

13. Go out for a drive to look at scenery

14. Make a picture or craft out of leaves, flowers or seashells

15. Go for a hike or bush walk

16. Bike riding

17. Grow herbs in a pot

18. Collect rocks

19. Visit a natural waterfall

20. Visit a national park

21. Listen to birds singing

22. Climb a tree

23. Count birds in the sky

24. Watch ants carry food

25. Make sand castles

26. Play with your pet dog or cat

27. Take photos of nature scenes

Action plan for a playful parent
90 ideas of playful activities to do
Tick those you might like to do

Activity	Tick	Activity	Tick	Activity	Tick
1. Finger paint		2. Do more connecting, play soccer, tennis, volleyball		3. Have a picnic at the park or on the lounge floor	
4. Make time to gaze at the stars at night		5. Helicopter spins		6. Make a book of Me and your family tree	
7. Use music to explore feelings, dance, sing and exercise		8. Play and make mazes		9. Counting and multiplying	
10. Explore new food ideas and tastes		11. Play board games		12. Blindfold guessing game	
13. Puppets to explore feelings		14. Visit museums and art galleries		15. Let's pretend game	
16. Hunt for numbers and exploring patterns		17. Learn fraction		18. Play shopping	
19. Explore butterflies and ants		20. Build with Lego		21. Make your own poem	
22. Do word puzzles		23. Read a recipe and bake a cake		24. Make a cubby house under the table or in the backyard	

Activity	Tick	Activity	Tick	Activity	Tick
25. Make an ant farm		26. Paint on canvas		27. Have a pyjama party	
28. Have a family games night		29. Make a recipe book of new and favourite meals		30. Make pottery	
31. Make model cars		32. Go for walks and talk		33. Have fun and draw members of the family	
34. Do more hugging and wrestling		35. Affirm your love with encouraging words, special gifts and special outings		36. Photographing artwork into their portfolio	
37. Make family rules together		38. Do a quiz and a riddle a day		39. Bean bag games	
40. Learn about countries and their favourite meals		41. Do miming and moving to illustrate a story		42. Identify all sounds in your environment	
43. Make things out of play dough		44. Your child as a TV producer		45. Learning about parts of the body and nutrition	
46. Weigh and measure everything		47. Learn shapes by feel		48. Explore trees or plants shapes, colour and design	
49. Explore a country of the month		50. Make your own calendar		51. Play home-made music, background music	

Activity	Tick	Activity	Tick	Activity	Tick
52. Go shopping for reading books for special reading box		53. Do mind mapping		54. Invite friends over	
55. Press flowers		56. Make something from cardboard boxes		57. Set up a tent and camp out in a tent in the backyard	
58. Go to the beach		59. Visit an art gallery or catch a ferry		60. Take photos and make a photo book	
61. Tell jokes and sing silly songs		62. Go to the park		63. Hike and fly kites at the park	
64. Do roll and tumble games		65. Read a variety of books from the library		66. Make a book of family activities	
67. List all the things your child can do and a list of things the child wants to do		68. Play bingo		69. Play ball games and balloon games	
70. Do an exercise plan with Brain Gym® every day, eye tracking activities, left/right activities (improves reading and learning)		71. Variations of 'I spy'		72. Play hide and seek	
73. Teach your children to draw		74. What comes next... storytelling		75. Using coins and board games for maths lessons	

Activity	Tick	Activity	Tick	Activity	Tick
76. Do maths in the kitchen		77. Hopscotch for counting		78. Make a garden and plant some seeds	
79. Explore magnets, levers, experimenting with friction and taking things apart		80. Read poetry		81. Dictating their own stories	
82. Visit the library		83. Play spelling games		84. Dress up and have a fashion show	
85. Write a letter to a friend or relative		86. Make a puppet show		87. Have a family movie night	
88. Go for a walk and talk		89. Go rock climbing		90. Play snap	

Be in the moment, listen to your child and have fun with them, as the first twelve years of life will go so fast.

Play is the highest form of RESEARCH
Albert Einstein

 Write your action plan ideas here.

CHAPTER 2

Step # 2: Recognise that your child is unique

"If we could look into each other's hearts and understand the unique challenges each of us faces, I think we would treat each other much more gently with more love, patience, tolerance and care."

Marvin J. Ashton

Accept and celebrate your child's uniqueness. Every child is unique in their own special way, like a snow flake or a finger print. Each child has a unique way of feeling, thinking, comprehending, and interacting with others. As a loving and nurturing parent, it's your job to encourage them to embrace their uniqueness and celebrate their individual qualities. Assist them to realise that they need not be concerned about being like 'everybody else'.

Our brains are the most remarkable information processing machines. Each of us, through biology and early childhood development, is gifted with unique neural wiring. We develop at different rates, have different learning styles, and excel more easily in some areas than others.

> *"When we watch youngsters at play, we can see what natural learners they are. Their curiosity impels them to sustain a particular point of focus-with both their attention and their whole body."*
> Dr. Paul Dennison from *'Brain Gym and Me: Reclaiming the pleasure of learning'*

Of course, our educational system is not designed to cope with unique individuals. Teaching and assessment is necessarily standardised, and children are taught from an early age to compete with their peers to be 'the best'. In this environment, poor performance leads to greater pressure, fear, and stress, which can inhibit effective learning. Self-esteem and the expectations in life are greatly influenced by the grades and rewards we receive in school. Poor performance at school can bring up negative emotions of the feelings of 'being dumb' and 'not good enough'. People learn differently.

> *"If the purpose for learning is to score well in a test, we have lost sight for the real reason for learning."*
> Jeannie Fulbright

Our ultimate aim is to become an integrated learner processing information using both hemispheres being 'switched on' at the same time. Being able to move and think at the same time and thrive on the new, the spontaneous and the creative. Learning is a joyful opportunity for full self-expression. Being able to move from receptive (right brain) to expressive (left brain) simultaneously.

> *"Every child has a limitless capability just waiting to blossom in its own way."*
>
> Dr Paul Dennison, *Brain Gym and Me:*
> *Reclaiming the pleasure of learning*

Does your child have learning disabilities – or just a different learning style?

When your child fails to achieve important educational milestones (such as learning to read) or does not perform well in standardised tests, a common response is to label them with learning disabilities and prescribe remedial classes to 'fix' the problem.

However, we are increasingly discovering that many children who are labelled with learning disabilities do not necessarily have limited capabilities; they simply have preferred learning styles that are not well supported within the traditional schooling system.

Carla Hannaford, a biologist, educator, and author of *Smart Moves* says,

> *"The health of our educational system depends on our nurturing and promoting the learning of all our citizens. We must relinquish judgements that lead to stress-provoking labels and competition. An appropriate thinking curriculum must be established that synthesises whole body/mind processing through regular art, music and movement in conjunction with*

cognitive skills. We must give learners body/mind integrative tools that allow them to stop the stress cycle and activate full sensory/hemisphere access. Perhaps then we can fully realise the unique human potential that Paul Maclean invokes, in an evolving society where all people succeed at learning.

People learn instinctively, but what we learn and how we view ourselves as learners very often depends on how we are treated by instructors and other role models in our life."

Understanding your child's learning style

We all recognise the diversity of human beings and each one of us is unique and interesting. Psychologists and educators have developed systems to identify these diversities. Systems such as Meyers-Briggs Index, Dunn's Learning Styles, Howard Gardner's Multiple Intelligences, Dominance Profiles, and other systems. Understanding these styles are helpful in planning and developing education and training programs to increase the learning potential of the learner. These systems are only a guide to help us understand our varied differences. It is important to honour each person for their giftedness. We are unique, gifted human beings with different learning styles influenced by experiences from our upbringing and environment. Labelling takes away the uniqueness and gifts that we individually have. We are continually growing and maturing. Life is about creating yourself.

How do we learn?

The brain is primarily a sensory processing machine that is constantly collecting and organising the information we receive from the world around us. This is how we experience, think, and learn. I've learned that two people can look at the exact same thing and see something totally different.

Therefore, all stages of learning development are shaped by how your child, as a unique individual, **best** collects information through their primary communication and learning senses – eyes (visual), ears (auditory), and movement (kinaesthetic).

We all require all three modes of learning for long term memory, yet your child usually has a natural preference towards one or two. These natural preferences particularly dominate when they are under stress – such as when they are exposed to new information or are experiencing learning difficulties.

Tell me and I'll forget,
Teach me and I'll remember.
Involve me and I'll learn
Ben Franklin

Move more and learn more

Brain Gym® and Rhythmic Movement Training are effective natural therapies and motor-sensory learning programs for better learning. Brain Gym® is the result of over 30 years of development by Paul E Dennison, Ph.D. and Gail E Dennison, pioneers in applied brain research. Rhythmic Movement Training was first devised in Sweden in the 1970s by a self-taught therapist Kerstin Linde. Dr Harald Blomberg, a Swedish psychiatrist used the reflex integration program in his practice with very good results. Both programs use exercises and techniques to reduce stress and activate the whole brain for optimal sensory perception, strengthen posture, central nervous system, memory, learning, emotions and behaviour. Further research has shown that muscular activities, especially coordinated balanced rhythmic movements appear to stimulate production of neurotropics that increase the number of new nerve cells and neural connections in the brain.

Dramatic Improvement

"My son was having difficulties in reading and writing, I thought by giving him extra work at home to practise on, it would help him to improve. Instead, he found it more difficult to cope with it. I read about Brain Gym® through a pamphlet explaining how it can help children with learning difficulties and I wanted to learn more about it. I went on the internet and came across Enza, who happened to be a qualified Brain Gym® Practitioner in the local area. I contacted her and brought my son in for the initial consultation and decided to have him do the Brain Gym® Program.

I've notice there has been a dramatic improvement in his spelling and comprehension skills. Before Brain Gym®, my son was getting 15/25 for spelling. By the time he had his second session, he was getting 23/25. He's now reading at a more fluent, faster pace. I was so delighted with the outcome of my son's progress."

Amy, Mother

Taylah's life changed

"Taylah, my eight year old daughter, was heading towards the end of year one. She was having difficulty with reading, writing, sounds, and generally being an uptight, easily upset, tired little girl. Learning was very slow and tiring for her. Her teacher would often say to me "Did Taylah have a late night?" My answer would always be "No", as bedtime was strictly 7.30pm. We later discovered that the reason for her tiredness was because it was

really hard work for her to concentrate on reading and writing and all the things kids need to do at school. She was simply so drained day after day. A visit to a behavioural optometrist showed her eyesight was fine, although her tracking and convergence were a problem, which the Kinesiologist had also picked up.

In desperation, I made an appointment with Enza, who was recommended to me by the visiting Kinesiologist to the school. It was a big commitment from us as we lived 3 hours from Enza and 1 session meant an all day trip.

After a few sessions, the commitment we made started to pay off. Taylah's whole outlook on life started to change. She began to be so much happier in herself and things that were once a huge drama now seemed to be behind her. I think because she was less uptight, other things started to fall in to place. Since starting the sessions with Enza, 7 months ago, Taylah has jumped up 10 levels in her reading, which is also more fluent. Her ability to do her daily journal entry at school has gone from "I can't do it" to writing nearly 2 pages some days and getting her ideas on paper much easier. Taylah's teacher also has been amazed by her changes these last few months in all areas of her schooling and within herself. The whole class now benefit from doing Brain Gym® and P.A.C.E exercises every morning and have really grown to love and enjoy it.

I'm so glad I started Taylah on this Brain Gym® journey as it gives her the tools to help her now and in the future. She is now a confident and happy little girl! Thank you, Enza, for all your help."

Belinda, Mother

Effective teaching

All children are natural learners, curious about everything in the world around them. They have complex and amazing brains, designed to make meanings and memories from their experiences. These experiences come into their brains through their bodily senses. Because each person has a slightly different brain, and different background and experiences, each person constructs meaning and memory in unique ways.

Effective, brain-friendly teaching allows students to process information in their own way, so they can build positive attitudes, strong memories, and the recall needed for successful results in their grades.

> *"Are we forming children who are only capable of learning what is already known? Or should we try to develop creative and innovative minds, capable of discovery from the preschool age on and throughout life?"*
>
> Jean Piaget

Understanding the learning styles

As learners, we can show preferences for some senses. Visual learners learn better by seeing things. Auditory learners prefer to hear about things. Kinaesthetic learners prefer to handle things. There are a host of learning preferences that people exhibit which contribute to your child's unique learning styles. For total whole-brain learning, we learn better by combining seeing, listening and doing.

As you read through the following section work out what your child's learning style is.

Visual communicators and learners collect information best by seeing

This may mean seeing pictures – incorporating memorable colours, shapes, and designs – or seeing words – focusing on how they are written or arranged. The visual communicator may have a problem mastering phonics when it comes to learning spelling. Flash cards are very effective for a visual learners. Many children have had huge improvements in spelling by simply making flash cards where they write the vowels in one colour and the consonants in another colour. Then, the parent says the word, while flashing the cards at the child's eye level. By using their photographic memory, the child remembers the words quickly and easily.

Auditory communicators and learners collect information best by listening and talking

They prefer to learn from lectures and recordings, and when spelling will 'sound out' words. The auditory communicator may find learning to read more difficult. They will learn well from stories, questions, audio tapes, talking to others and self, discussions and debates.

Kinaesthetic communicators and learners collect information best through movement and action

They enjoy dancing and sport, and will fidget, gesture, and give messages through touch. The kinaesthetic communicator may find it difficult to sit still and concentrate during talks and blackboard lessons. These children like to doodle with a pen on paper, squeeze a soft ball or sit on a gym ball while listening. They need to move in order to learn. They need practical experiences, real or imaginary, at the start of anything. Movement anchors their thought.

The purpose of dominance profiles

Knowing your child's dominance profile will help you understand why your child sometimes acts in a certain way and has difficulty performing certain tasks. When a child is learning in a safe supported environment they can excel in learning. When under stress they can get a learning block. For example a child trying very hard and bogged down in details to write down or communicate their thoughts, will lose access to their creative right brain, thus having difficulties fully communicating their thoughts and ideas. This child may be leading with his left brain rather than using his whole brain.

Carla Hannaford, a biologist, educator, and author of Smart Moves states that:

> *"When we are under stress, we rely most on our dominant senses and our preferred ways of processing. In less stressful situations, our dominance profiles can fluctuate. . . . When we are confronted with a new learning situation, we will access information most easily through our dominant senses (eyes or ears), and express (either verbally, with gestures or in writing) with our dominant hand. Because of our innate neural circuitry, the left hemisphere controls movement and receives sensory information from the right side of the body. The right hemisphere controls movement and receives sensory information from the left side of the body."*

Some people's brains work better with small step-by-step details to build a big picture (left brain processing), while others prefer to understand general ideas, the big picture first, and then fill in the details (right brain processing).

Holistic learners lead with the right brain

Many children are whole picture learners. They need overviews and contexts before they can begin working or fitting data into their own thinking. They need to know "what does this mean for me?" "how does this fit in?" or "where is this leading?" Those who lead with the right brain tend to be able to take in the big image, feel the emotional connections, access intuitive understanding, and are spontaneous and learn kinaesthetically through movement. They access art, music, singing, sports, dance, and drama with a passion. Many of these children struggle through the education system, as they are not taught by their learning style. They become stressed and labelled as special needs students or learning disabled. This learning style is not fully appreciated in the school system.

Analytic learners lead with the left

This style is more valued by the school system. They often are high achievers academically in the traditional classrooms, yet they are usually a small percentage. I have found many of these children experience anxiety because of the pressures of societal, parental, and their own expectations to achieve to a certain standard. Analytic learners are step-by-step logical thinkers. They like lists, facts, details, organising things, and finishing them properly. Many children who are labelled gifted and talented tend to lead with the left brain.

Underdevelopment or overstimulation of one hemisphere, either left or right, with the exclusion of the other, leads to a breakdown in optimal brain processing. The key element is to be able to use the left and right simultaneously, working together effectively to easily process information.

Introducing Brain Gym® exercises and Rhythmic Movement Training in the home and the classrooms will assist all students to learn more easily through movement.

We are all different, but our schools are not

The reality is that traditional schooling favours auditory learners, because the teacher, particularly in higher grades, conveys information through lecturing. Visual learning is also important for reading and studying textual information. Kinaesthetic learners, although they may do well at sports, are likely to miss out in the classroom. Including Brain Gym® movements and practical hands-on activities can make the difference and improve their learning.

Carla Hannaford, a biologist and educator, was involved in using dominance profile assessments in many schools with many students, and she began to see certain patterns emerge. In her book, 'Smart Moves', she says:

> "I noticed, for example, that many of the students who were gestalt brain hemisphere dominant and/or sensory limited were also the ones who had been labelled as having learning difficulties. In 1990, I undertook a more formal study to compare dominance profile types with schools' system of labelling students. . . . In the past 14 years I have continued the dominance profile research and consistently found the same patterns. . . . In the schools I studied, students with high verbal abilities and logic brain processing were more often labelled gifted and talented. Those with gestalt processing and low linear verbal skills were more frequently labelled as learning disabled/Special Education."

The key approach to equipping your child for success

No learning style is inherently superior. By understanding where your child's strengths lay, you can help them develop their complimentary communication and learning skills through targeted exercises and techniques, such as Brain Gym®. By using their full range of senses they activate more of their brain and achieve better performance.

The key is to maximise all of the brain pathways which allow for whole brain learning in order to utilise all your child's learning styles.

Most importantly, your child does not need to feel there is something wrong with them. Such negative feelings only add to their stress and exacerbate their learning difficulties. So, before your child is labelled with learning disabilities, consider opportunities to work with their strengths and learning styles, so they can truly switch-on for success.

From her book, *'The Dominance Factor'*, Carla Hannaford explains:

> *"The optimal learning state is one of whole-brain integration. In this state, both hemispheres are equally active all the time, thus accessing all sensory information and effectively communicating, moving and acting on the information. The learning environment can be designed or improved to encourage whole-brain learning. For one thing, the setting should be stimulating, but as stress-free as possible. As mentioned previously, stress increases unilateral functioning. Additionally, learners should be offered a broad spectrum of multi-sensory opportunities. If they can see visual presentation, hear auditory explanations, and get tactile opportunities to touch and take apart models, manipulatives, etc., there's a greater chance of*

matching all students' learning preferences. Another important ingredient of successful learning is the opportunity to move frequently – both to wake up the brain and to anchor learning.

A wide range of activities can be highly effective in anchoring learning into the mind/body system. Among them are Brain Gym®, Eurhythmics, Tai Chi singing alone or in groups, self-created music and dance sessions, cooperative (non-competitive) physical education programs, self and group-expressive art activities, cooperative group solution finding, and quiet reflective time."

You can teach
a student a lesson
for a day;
but if you can teach
him to learn by
creating curiosity
he will continue the
learning processing as long as he lives
Anonymous

Seven intelligences

At Harvard University, Howard Gardner developed the theory of 'multiple intelligences'. With far-reaching implications for education, it states that each of us has the potential to develop at least seven different intelligences.

Linguistic intelligence: This is the ability to communicate with language—reading, speaking, and writing.

Mathematical-logical intelligence: This is the ability to reason, think logically, and calculate.

Visual-spatial intelligence: This is the ability to draw, paint, take great photos, create sculptures, or to visualise spaces.

Musical intelligence: This is the ability to write songs and poetry, play musical instruments, and sing.

Interpersonal intelligence: This is the ability to get along with others and involves sharing, teaching, and collaboration.

Intra-personal intelligence: This is the ability to reflect, access your feelings, intuition, and make plans.

Bodily-physical intelligence: This is the ability to use one's physical body or hands, and includes exercise, dance, and movement.

Others believe there are even more intelligence traits. For example, visual ability and spatial ability are not necessarily connected. Someone may be artistically talented, yet wouldn't be able to find his way back to a hotel in a strange city. The Gardner model provides us with a good working picture of intelligence. It helps us realise the vital need to provide opportunities to let talent show itself. And most importantly, to develop all the intelligences to provide a strong base for our child's future skills.

Therefore, we are to stimulate the brain pathways on which ALL types of future abilities are based.

> If a child cannot learn
> the way we teach,
> Maybe we could teach
> the way they learn.

Action Plan to develop and encourage your child's love for learning

Make sure that your child has the opportunity to grow in an environment which provides the widest possible range of experiences! Music, singing and dancing of all types, gymnastics, sports, travelling to new places and countries, speaking different languages, nature, arts and crafts and other forms of creativity, as well as situations that will lead to a rich vocabulary and a love of reading, writing and mathematics.

Write your action plan ideas here.

CHAPTER 3

Step #3: Give them what they need to grow

"I have never heard of a flower with Attention Deficit Hyperactivity Disorder. If a flower isn't growing we give it what it needs: water, nutrition, sunlight, patience and love."
Paul E. Dennison PhD, Creator of Brain Gym®

Turbo-charge your child's learning

A simple substance that we ingest daily can make our brain work better, boost our energy levels, and increase our concentration.

This amazing liquid is useful in turbo-charging your child's classroom learning, and can do the same for you at work. It is a totally natural remedy for education, is freely and readily available, and is part one of a four step process used in Brain Gym® programs to prepare children for learning.

It's water!

How important is water?

Each of our bodies is composed of more than 45 percent water, some 65 percent of our body weight. Thinner people have a greater percentage of water to body weight—one more reason to drink lots of water. Most important of all, our brain is composed of 85% water.

Water is vital for a wide range of critical bodily functions and a lack of adequate water can lead to problems. In fact, simply drinking one to two glasses of clean filtered water in the morning can help your child succeed in class and get better grades by helping with:

> ➢ Oxygen delivery to the brain and rest of the body

> ➢ Aiding digestion and energy distribution

> ➢ Flushing harmful toxins and removing wastes from the body

> ➢ Improving nerve communications

All these functions are critical to our health and well-being, so encouraging your child to drink lots of water, every day, is not only important for their schoolwork, but their overall health as well.

How much water is enough?

It is recommended that adults drink between eight and twelve glasses per day. Children are half the size of adults and require approximately half of adult requirements. The amount of water varies depending on the weight, height, and the type of activities children and adults are involved in. During times of high outdoor heat, extended physical activity, or periods of emotional distress, it is vital to add additional water to your diet.

Teach your children not to wait until their brain signals that they are thirsty - by that time they are probably already becoming dehydrated. If we ignore such messages from our brain, we are telling our body it isn't important, which means our brain may not send out the necessary alert-to-thirst sensation messages the next time we are dehydrated. We may not even feel thirsty. This, of course, can be dangerous.

Staying hydrated is easy if you set up a plan for your child to drink water regularly throughout the day. Have your child take a refillable stainless steel, BPA free or glass bottle to school or when out and about and keep on his desk. At the end of the day check how much the child has drunk.

Be alert to the following signs of thirst in your child, which you may never have connected with dehydration in the past:

> ➢ Constantly seems tired and has trouble rising in the morning

> ➢ Lack of focus and easily bored

> ➤ Seems confused or drowsy many times

> ➤ Complains of stomach aches, headaches, and muscle cramps

Be smart and hydrate

An article from the Daily Mail, Courier Mail 18 July, 2013 explained how research shows that drinking water can sharpen the mind. The effects are particularly marked if a person is thirsty. Researchers at the University of East London believe that once thirst is relieved, the brain is able to focus.

To illustrate this, they carried out an experiment on thirty-four men and women who twice completed a number of mental tests – once after a breakfast of just a cereal bar and again after a cereal bar with a bottle of water.

The journal, *Frontiers in Human Neuroscience*, reported their findings, noting that all participants were asked whether they were thirsty or not at the time of testing. Of those who said they weren't thirsty, equally quick reaction test times, with or without the water, resulted. However, those who stated they were thirsty pre-testing had quicker reaction test times after having a drink, up to 14 per cent quicker.

The researchers think the addition of drinking water helped to free up the parts of the brain that were busy telling the body it was thirsty.

Water, just plain water!

Many people think that drinking lots of soft drinks, tea, or coffee will fulfil their water needs. Nothing could be further from the truth!

Caffeine in all of these drinks is a diuretic, meaning it leaches water from the body and from your brain. Additionally, high sugar content juices and soft drinks are identified by the body's systems as food, so it draws water from your body to help you digest them, dehydrating you still further. You can see how easily we can dehydrate ourselves without realising it.

If your child struggles with school work and reading, the very first thing is to check if they are drinking enough water. Supply them with sufficient water to help hydrate them fully.

Eating wrong foods can harm your brain

Scientists are beginning to find that eating the wrong foods can harm your brain as well as many other bodily functions. The flip side to this is that adding some foods that we know give the brain lots of nourishment can literally turn a child around. Common sense dictates that improving the health of the brain can only be beneficial.

Our brain cells are nutritionally demanding and complex, but when the proper foods are provided to children to nourish their brains and their body, it helps activate their true learning potential. The old saying *we are what we eat* is fairly true.

It is important to feed your children a variety of healthy meals and snacks. Avoid feeding children highly processed, high sugar, high fat junk food, which will only contribute to obesity and malnutrition. Using junk food as a treat can also teach the wrong message. Give children healthy snacks as treats.

It is vital to supply children with the right types of energy. Children need to eat before school and obtain enough protein foods for growth, as well as lots of fruits and vegetables that are filled with the vitamins and minerals needed for optimal health.

Teach your children the importance of a proper diet and set the example by eating properly yourself. If children see you eat junk food on a regular basis, while you are telling them to eat healthy foods, they will see you as a hypocrite. Encourage your children to make the right food choices by being the role model. Eating together gives your family the time to connect and you have more control over what foods your family eats. Having the TV off at meal times really helps.

Many families have busy schedules these days. If you choose to have a pizza delivered occasionally, order something with beef or chicken with more vegetables served with a side salad to make the pizza meal healthier.

Brain stressors

Our brain is very complex and it interacts with every other system in the body. Therefore, it is vital to understand the connection between eating unhealthy foods and how it affects the brain. Foods with high fat, high sugar, and low nutritional value, such as fast foods and packaged, processed snacks that can be left on shelves for months, are to be avoided as if your life depended on it - because it truly does.

Chemicals in our foods and tap water are also a huge problem nowadays; additives, colourants, preservatives, pollen, dust mites, mould, heavy metals, and pesticide contamination may all be present. Likewise, products we use for household cleaning, cosmetics, and personal care are filled with chemicals. Many plastic containers leach chemicals like Xenoestrogens and other chemicals into our food, which may be capable of causing future health problems. Fragrances, perfumes, and wood products like particle board, plywood glues, insulation materials, carpeting and furniture give off various potentially noxious gasses. Formaldehyde, a colourless, strong-smelling chemical, is also used on imported clothing, nail polish, wood products, glues, adhesives, insulation materials, and many other products. Cancers, diabetes, overweight problems, auto-immune diseases, and many other diseases are on the increase. Could it be from chemicals and toxins?

I have come across some interesting information on how these chemicals are affecting our health and well-being, and that there are ways to reduce some of the effects of these toxins:

The *State of the Science of Endocrine Disrupting Chemicals—2012*

Edited by Åke Bergman, Jerrold J. Heindel, Susan Jobling, Karen A. Kidd and R. Thomas Zoeller

This paper is an update of the scientific knowledge, including main conclusions and key concerns, on endocrine disruptors as part of the ongoing collaboration between the World Health Organization (WHO) and the United Nations Environment Programme (UNEP) to address concerns about the potential adverse health effects of chemicals on humans and wildlife.

We live in a world in which man-made chemicals have become a part of everyday life. It is clear that some of these chemical pollutants can affect the endocrine (hormonal) system, and certain of these endocrine disruptors may also interfere with the developmental processes of humans and wildlife species. Following international recommendations in 1997 by the Intergovernmental

Forum on Chemical Safety and the Environment Leaders of the Eight regarding the issue of endocrine disrupting chemicals (EDCs), WHO, through the International Programme on Chemical Safety (IPCS), a joint programme of WHO, UNEP and the International Labour Organization, developed in 2002 a report entitled *Global Assessment of the State-of-the-Science of Endocrine Disruptors.*

Invisible Killers: The Truth About Environmental Genocide Hardcover – June 8, 2007

By Rik J. Deitsch and Stewart Lonky, M.D.

The book educates readers about the very real dangers that surround us every day in the air we breathe, the water we drink, and the foods we eat. These environmental toxins can build up in our bodies, causing disease and even death. Rik Deitsch and Dr. Stewart Lonky identify the problems and offer solutions that will help you reduce the toxic burden for your family, and live a healthier, longer life.

Go natural

Always check the ingredients on food and product labels to avoid ingesting or coming into contact with these chemicals. Go natural whenever possible, use natural products inside your home for cleaning products, cosmetics, as well as furniture and personal care items. Increase ventilation in your home and add some potted plants. Invest in a good quality water filter for clean drinking water.

Glassware, ceramic, stainless steel, and stoneware cooking utensils are preferable. Again, scientists have made connections between hyperactivity in children and the presence of toxic metals like lead, cadmium, and mercury in the body. High levels of manganese, copper, and iron also seem to pose problems, while deficiencies of some essential minerals can lead to decreased brain function - more likely if there is heavy metal overload and can be as debilitating, especially in children.

Electromagnetic fields

Natural and man-made electromagnetic fields (EMF's) are present everywhere in our environment. Short term affects could be headaches, being unable to concentrate, or poor sleeping habits. Common EMF emitters in your home are things such as cordless phones, mobile phones, televisions, computers, Wi-Fi, digital smart metres, and certain types of electrical appliances. Reduce the number of electrical appliances in your child's bedroom and switch them off at the wall (or unplug) at bedtime to reduce the EMF effects on their bodies while sleeping. If possible, always choose hard-wired over wireless appliances, especially home computer systems.

Researchers have established a compelling link between gut bacteria and mental health

In the United States, a Boston-area psychiatrist, James Greenblatt, has adopted a surprising approach besides psychotherapy and medication. He prescribes probiotics (bacteria that live in the gut) to patients who have been diagnosed with severe cases of obsessive compulsive disorder (OCD), as well as ADHD. By prescribing daily doses of probiotics there have been miraculous changes in patients' illnesses.

Dr Greenblatt has dedicated his professional career to using integrated psychiatry to treat mental illness. He employs both medical and complementary therapies to help his patients function better to achieve their personal goals. He integrates medical and natural therapies into the treatment of psychiatric disorders.

Greenblatt says he was perplexed by the way mental disorders were treated, as if the brain was totally separate from the body. He expressed this in the following statement: *"Each year I get more and more impressed at how important the gastrointestinal tract is for healthy mood and the controlling of behaviour."*

Probiotics help detoxify the body and reduce stress. Getting your gastrointestinal tract healthy and keeping it that way can help avoid problems like fatigue, irritability, poor coordination, mood swings, joint and muscle pain, memory problems, and sleeping difficulties. It is worth considering this factor if your child has any of these symptoms.

Here are some of the things that can cause a leaky gut: severe emotional stress or trauma, use of antibiotics, lack of probiotics, ingestion of junk foods (fried foods and sugar laden foods), gastro-intestinal parasites, intestinal bacterial infections, and candida over-growth and nutritional deficiencies.

Dr Cryan, a neuroscientist at the University of Cork in Ireland, and a main investigator at the Alimentary Pharmabiotic Centre, led a study where anxious mice dosed with the probiotic bacterium Lactobacillus rhamnosus (JB-1) showed lower levels of anxiety, decreased stress hormones, and even an increase in brain receptors for a neurotransmitter that is vital in curbing worry, anxiety, and fear.

Probiotics are friendly bacteria that can neutralise toxins and stabilise the gastrointestinal tract, ultimately improving the immune system. Many people think yogurt will fix the problem. Yogurt is a great food, if you are not milk intolerant. Unfortunately, the friendly bacteria yogurt provides does not survive in the gastrointestinal tract. The body has to be continually replenished with the friendly bacteria. It is easier and more effective to supplement with probiotic capsules daily. Check at the store for good quality probiotic capsules or powders, with at least 8 different strains of probiotic that deliver longer lasting benefits and can be regularly incorporated into your diet.

Nourishing your child's brain, and your own

For optimal health and good brain functioning and performance, the best diet is one filled with fresh, natural foods, a variety of fruits and vegetables, high quality proteins, whole grains, nuts, legumes, calcium sources, and healthy oils, like olive and coconut.

Phytochemicals found in vegetables and whole grains are critical for optimal brain functioning and help to ward off disease. Many people lack enough phytochemicals in their diets. Supplementing your diet with fresh green vegetable juice or green food extract in powder or capsule form is one way to ensure you aren't lacking in phytochemicals.

One of the best food supplements that contains all the minerals our body needs is *Algotene*, a red marine Phytoplankton, also called whole dried *Dunaliella salina*, which is grown in Australia. A pilot study made on heavy-metal chelation using marine micro-algae, showed impressive outcomes from whole dried *Dunaliella salina*. The major aim of this study was to determine the effectiveness of this micro-algae in elevating the blood serum carotenoid levels and the chelating effects, and the detoxification of toxic minerals and heavy metals. The results after 12 weeks showed that the whole dried *Dunaliella salina* cells significantly elevated blood serum carotenoid levels in all participants. Tissue samples showed significant reductions in the levels of heavy metals and toxic elements across participants as well as improvements in nutritional balances.

Many of my clients sing praises for this product, commenting on their increased energy, mental clarity, reduced effects of PMS and hot flushes in menopause, and a boost to their immune system during colds and flues. It is extremely useful for detoxification, which removes heavy metals from the body. Check my website for more information on Algotene, *(Dunaliella salina)* at Enza's Store.

Omega-three fatty acids and omega-six fatty acids are widely known as brain power foods. In addition, your child needs plenty of calcium, iron, zinc, magnesium, and B vitamins. Hair tissue analysis can give you a blueprint of what supplements you might need to give your child. It tests for dozens of minerals and nutrients and reports if they are at the proper level, or which ones are lacking or are excessively high or toxic. To find out more about Hair Tissue Mineral Analysis, please download the forms and contact me on my website.

Eliminate and cleanse

As noted earlier, plenty of clean, filtered water is absolutely essential for the brain and the body to have optimal health, as water takes nutrition to the cells and removes toxins from the body.

Finally, be sure that your child's gastrointestinal tract functions well to remove waste and toxicity from the body. Eliminating parasites in your gut, and your child's, can improve the immune system and overall health of the family.

Small amounts of colloidal silver has been used by many people for hundreds of years to eliminate most parasites and unfriendly bacteria and fungi in the body. Give it to your pet animals in their water to stop the spread of parasites to your children. Before the 1930s there were electronic devices to make colloidal silver to assist in eliminating parasites and bacteria in the blood.

There are so many natural complementary medicines to assist you in maintaining good health for the family. Chinese herb supplements work well. Oregano oil is effective in improving digestion and eliminating parasites. Zeolite, a volcanic mineral, assists in removing chemicals and heavy metals from the body. Products called Natural Cellular Defence or Mega Defense are also effective in improving the immune system and removing heavy metals, pesticides, and chemicals out of the body. Research what works best for you and your family and contact me if you would like more information on such products.

What foods and products to eliminate or restrict

Many children are allergic or have sensitivities to foods like soy, dairy, eggs, sugar, wheat, corn, shellfish, chocolate, or peanuts. Watch for signs of food allergies and eliminate any problem foods from their diet.

Additionally, avoid preservatives and food additives, including artificial sweeteners like saccharin, aspartame, and Splenda, MSG, food dyes, nitrates, and any other unknown chemicals you read on the packaging. Keep them out of your child's diet to the greatest extent possible for their health and well-being.

Genetically modified, engineered foods are another challenge. There is much debate about genetically modified foods not being safe and having less nutrition. Avoid them, if you can. They have been banned in many countries.

Vaccinations are another area about which there is much debate on the potential for causing death, allergies, and health problems.

Why has there been an increase in Autism, Celiac disease, Diabetes, Crones disease, Asthma, and a whole host of food allergies by more than 300% since 1996? Is it all the chemicals that are stored in our cells so that our immune system is becoming overstimulated? What is causing a poor immune system?

Heavy metal exposure

Arizona State University (ASU) researchers conducted studies published in the journal, *Biological Trace Element Research,* suggesting that heavy metal exposure may be a cause of autism. The researchers found that autistic children had significantly higher levels of numerous toxic metals in their blood than non-autistic children.

Autism is a neurological disorder that causes repetitive or restricted behaviour and trouble with communication and social interaction. According to the *Centres for Disease Control and Prevention* (CDC), it affects one in every 252 girls and one in every 54 boys in the United States. Although mainstream medicine long considered autism to be a hereditary disorder, increasing evidence is emerging that links the condition to various environmental factors, such as toxic exposure.

> *"Studies such as this improve our understanding,"* said Caroline Hattersley of the UK-based *National Autism Society*, adding that further studies should be performed to back up this research.

More exposure equals more severe symptoms

The ASU researchers tested blood and urinary levels of various toxic heavy metals in ninety-nine children between the ages of five and fifteen. Fifty-five of the children had autism, while forty-four did not. The groups were similar in age and gender distributions.

The researchers found that autistic children had 41 percent higher levels of lead in their blood and 74 percent higher levels in their urine than non-autistic children. Their urinary levels of tungsten were 44 percent higher, thallium levels were 77 percent higher, and tin levels were 115 percent higher. The researchers noted that all four of these metals have previously been linked with impaired brain function and development, and can be toxic to other organ systems as well.

Based on three separate scales of autism severity, the researchers also found that higher blood levels of toxic metals were associated with more severe cases of autism. In fact, between 38 and 47 percent of all variation in autism severity could be explained by varying heavy metal levels, particularly cadmium and mercury. This made toxic metal burden the single "strongest factor" predicting severity, the researchers said.

The findings come as no surprise, given the well-established neurotoxic effects of heavy metal exposure.

> *"We knew that exposure to lead makes people lose IQ points, and clearly it can induce autism,"* lead researcher, James Adams said. *"The study also showed that people with the highest levels are least able to excrete them."*

The findings may have real-world implications for both preventing and treating autism, however.

> *"We hypothesize that reducing early exposure to toxic metals may help ameliorate symptoms of autism, and treatment to remove toxic metals may reduce symptoms of autism,"* the researchers wrote. *"These hypotheses need further exploration, as there is a growing body of research to support it."* 'Autistic children have more toxic metals in their blood', posted by Newzfeed on March 15th, 2013

I have found that products like Natural Cellular Defence, Algotene or Mega Defense are effective in improving the immune system and nourishing the body, because these products have been found through hair analysis to remove heavy metals, pesticides, and chemicals from the body.

This research supports eating organically fresh grown whole foods for the greatest part of your family's diet. Over sixty years ago, people had their own vegetable gardens and fruit trees in their backyard. Their home-grown food was approximately 80 percent of their diet. When growing up on the farm, my parents grew most of our food and prepared all our meals. We had delicious home prepared and home cooked meals every day. There were no take-away restaurants down the road when I was growing up. Today, it is so easy to get take-away, yet it could be hazardous to your family's health because of the artificial flavours, colours, preservatives and other unknown chemicals. Small amounts of these chemicals ingested every day accumulate in the body over a life time.

Start to grow some of your food in your own vegetable garden and fruit trees in your backyard or in pots on your patio. Children love to pick strawberries and fruit from the trees or delicious pea pods from the vine or pull carrots from the ground. As young children, we used to enjoy going to the chicken pen and being able to play with the chickens and collect the eggs.

Healthy foods

Many healthful food choices abound – rice, rolled oats, buckwheat, millet, whole grains and flours, fruits and vegetables grown without pesticides, fish, nuts, beans, seeds, meat and poultry. Honey, maple syrup, coconut sugar, and stevia are good sweeteners to use. High fibre foods like vegetables, fruits, and whole grains are great for sweeping toxins out of our bodies. For example, for breakfast make smoothies with your child's favourite fruit, such as bananas or berries with whey, yogurt or protein powder. Green drink smoothies are very nutritious with green leafy vegetables mixed with beetroot and carrot. These foods are high in antioxidants. Experiment and make them tasty. Blenders or juicers are a great investment and produce healthy juices very quickly. Be creative and give your child the best healthy foods you can put together.

Make meal time fun

Be creative and introduce many varieties of food in your weekly menu. Plan a week or two ahead of time. Cook double the amount of food for a meal and freeze half of it for another day when you are short of time. Having an extra freezer is a great investment to provide more storage space. Then, you can prepare home-cooked healthy, tasty meals in advance to save you time and money.

Teach children to eat real, fresh nutritious foods instead of quick, processed foods. You do not know what type of ingredients, such as oils, sugars, salts, preservatives, artificial flavours and chemicals are in take-away foods that could be causing your child's reactions, allergies, and even weight problems.

Have fun with the whole family by planning, preparing, and cooking meals together. There are so many interesting recipes in books and on the internet. Plan ahead of time so your family can have healthy meals every day. Making a recipe book with all the family's favourite meals can be lots of fun.

Action Plan for building a healthy body and mind

Good Nutrition Ideas

All parents want their children to be healthy. Good nutrition not only makes a child physically healthy, it also makes your child emotionally more stable and improve school performance. Paying attention to their diet has high rewards.

Place massive amounts of love and joy in preparing your food for the family. Coming from an Italian family background, I have wonderful memories of family get-togethers without television and mobile phones. Delicious meals bring about emotional enjoyment, happy connections, and fond memories. That's why we often crave certain meals, because happy childhood memories are connected to that food. Likewise, unhappy experiences can give negative reactions to food. Do your best to prepare delicious meals that nourish your family to build healthy bodies and happy memories.

Breakfast

When your children wake up in the morning, they have gone over twelve hours without food. Your children are hungry, whether they realise it or not. A nutritious breakfast will provide energy for several hours until lunch. A doughnut or bowl of cereal will give your child a quick rush of energy that will last about 40 minutes, but is not enough nutrition to last until morning break.

Make breakfast nutritious by offering a variety of options:

> ➢ Blend a smoothie with un-homogenised full cream milk (cow, goat, almond milk or water) mixed with vanilla, yogurt or whey powder and honey or stevia. With the smoothies, add a variety of fruits like bananas, berries or other favourite fruit.

➢ Soak overnight or cook cereal like rolled oats, rice, millet and add nuts or sunflower seeds, raisins or fresh fruit.

➢ Heat up and eat leftovers from the meal the night before.

➢ Layer yogurt, fruit and granola in glasses for a parfait look.

➢ A breakfast buffet with sliced fresh fruits or finger food vegetables, hard-boiled eggs, scrambled eggs, or pancakes, zucchini quiche, omelette with cheese, whole-wheat blueberry muffins, or nut balls. The more colourful the better. Children love variety.

Lunch

Packing lunch boxes with fresh nutritious delicious foods can be challenging. Be creative, so it isn't tossed in the garbage bins at school or traded away for other children's food or simply not eaten and replaced with bought processed food at the cafeteria. However, school cafeterias are beginning to make available healthy nutritious food for students. Children need lots of minerals, vitamins, proteins, and complex carbohydrates in order to build healthy body and mind.

➢ Fresh fruits are nutritious and need no preparation.

➢ Mix a punnet of yogurt with applesauce, crushed pineapple, berries or chopped dates.

➢ Sunflower seeds, dried fruits and coconut shavings, packed or dried fruit, seeds, cereal blended and rolled into a ball in coconut

➢ Tuna or salmon with sliced cucumbers, grated carrots, celery, sprouts

➤ Eggs – hard boiled, zucchini or spinach quiche, muffins, curried egg sandwiches

➤ Pancakes and crepes

➤ Cheese and salad sandwiches

➤ Home cooked popcorn

➤ Vegetable sticks like carrot, celery, capsicum, cucumber, and broccoli served with hummus, cheese stick or slices

➤ Whole wheat, rice crackers or gluten free crackers served with a variety of toppings such as soft cheeses like ricotta, cottage cheese, sliced cheese, hummus or vegetable dip

➤ Left overs from evening meals

➤ Stir-fried rice served with egg and vegetables

➤ Home-made cheese cake, apple and blueberry pie, blueberry, chocolate or vegetable muffins

➤ Sandwiches cut into different shapes with a cookie cutter.

Dinner

Evening meals are best if planned ahead of time. After a busy day at work, you will feel tired and less likely to want to prepare meals and may be more likely to order take-away meals. It is important to plan and prepare evening meals on the weekends. Involve your children and have fun cooking together. Here are some ideas to help you plan your favourite meals. Most of these meals can be cooked ahead of time on the weekend and placed in the freezer.

➤ Beef, chicken or bean casseroles cooked in a slow cooker

➤ Rice dishes

➤ Pasta dishes like spaghetti, lasagne and ravioli (either whole meal or gluten free)

➤ Meatloaf or vegetarian loaf

➤ Beef, chicken or lentil rissoles

➤ Roast chicken, lamb, beef or fish

➤ Healthy pizzas with a variety of healthy ingredients to make your own gourmet pizza

➤ Soups with a variety of ingredients like pumpkin soup, vegetable soup, lentil soup, chicken and corn soup

➤ Make a batch of mince for tacos, rice or pasta

➤ Home-made meat, chicken or vegetable pies

➤ Fruit pies such as apple and blueberry pie

➤ Home-made ice cream or frozen fruit yogurt

➤ Quiche made with spinach, asparagus, chicken or zucchini

➤ Home-made cheese cake, carrot cake, banana cake, blueberry muffins or vegetable muffins

The recipes are endless. There is so much more. Have fun and research in recipe books and on the internet to find what you like.

On a week day, before you go to work, take out a prepared meal for the evening to defrost during the day in the refrigerator. Avoid the microwave and use the conventional oven, as there is still much debate about the safety of microwave. In the evening, simply warm up the meal in the oven to serve with steamed vegetables, wholegrain rice or fresh green salad to make a complete healthy meal. Lunch boxes can be packed the next day with left overs or small, divided portions of the prepared food from the freezer served with fresh fruit and chopped up carrot, celery, and cheese sticks.

Proper balanced nutrition can make incredible differences to your child; they can become healthier, calmer, more optimistic and happy, responsive to learning new things, and able to focus much better. It is so vital to teach your children how to enjoy cooking tasty, healthy, and delicious home cooked meals.

Family meals have a major influence on your child's nutrition, education and communication.

The Original Fast Food

Teach your children
to eat real foods
Not fast processed, high-sugar, high-fat food
Not junk food
Just fresh, alive, nutritious,
WHOLESOME HEALTHY FOOD.

 Write down the foods that are to be eliminated in your family's diet

 Write down the healthy meals you would like to add to your family's diet

Work out your weekly meal planner

Time	Sunday	Monday	Tuesday	Wednesday	Thursday	Friday	Saturday
Breakfast							
Snack							
Lunch							
Snack							
Dinner							

 Write your action plan ideas here.

CHAPTER 4

Step # 4: Empower your children to be their 'best selves'

Everything We Need Is Already Inside Us

When we plant a rose in the earth, we notice that it is small,
but we do not criticise it as "rootless and stem less."
We treat it as a seed, giving it the water and nourishment
required of a seed. When it first shoots up out of the earth,
we don't condemn it as immature and underdeveloped;
nor do we criticise the buds for not being open when they appear.
We stand in wonder at the process taking place
and give the plant the care it needs at each stage of development.
The rose is a rose from the time it is a seed to the time it dies.
Within it, at all times, it contains its whole potential.
It seems to be constantly in the process of its whole potential.
It seems to be constantly in the process of change;
yet at each stage, at each moment
it is perfectly all right as it is.

Author Unknown

You cannot spoil your child by loving them too much. Being well-loved by the person that you love most is vital to building self-esteem, and one of the most basic parts of your child's development. Babies who are well cared for feel warm, comfortable, and content based on their experiences with people and their environment. Parents can create an environment that the make children feel good about themselves.

Self-esteem means self-value and it is vital for children, because they feel proud of who they are and things that they do. It gives them confidence and courage to do new things and helps them develop respect for themselves, encouraging others to respect them as well.

Healthy self-esteem is a child's armour against the challenges of the world. Children who feel good about themselves seem to have an easier time handling conflicts and resisting negative pressures. They are generally optimistic and smile more readily and enjoy life. Children who feel important are well-rounded, respectful, and excel in academics. They also develop healthy relationships with their peers.

People who love to learn and are successful generally have good self-esteem. Most babies are born with good self-esteem, yet their self-esteem may not develop properly if not nurtured. If their life is very hard, and people they love are rough on them, self-esteem can all but disappear.

Nurturing from conception

Dr. Thomas R Verny MD, psychiatrist, writes in *Pre-Parenting: Nurturing Your Child from Conception,* "It makes a difference whether we are conceived in love, haste or hate, and whether a mother wants to be pregnant...parents do better when they live in a calm and stable environment free of addictions and supported by family and friends."

Research is showing how important parents' attitudes are in the development of the fetus. Again Dr. Verny writes: "In fact, the great weight of the scientific evidence that has emerged over the last decade demands that we reevaluate the mental and emotional abilities of unborn children. Awake or asleep, the studies show, the unborn children are constantly tuned in to their mother's every action, thought and feeling. From the moment of conception, the experience in the womb shapes the brain and lays the groundwork for personality, emotional temperament, and the power of higher thought."

The importance of the father's role in the healthy development of children

Children with involved, caring fathers have better educational outcomes. Several studies have shown that fathers who are involved, nurturing, and playful with their infants have children with higher IQ's, as well as better linguistic and cognitive capacities. When a father has a good relationship with the mother of his children, he sets an important example for his children. When they witness affectionate, respectful, and unconditional love between the mother and father, children are more likely to be happy and well-adjusted.

Fathers have a direct impact on the well-being of their children. Many studies have shown that children who have close positive relationships with their fathers have higher self-esteem and confidence. Widowed or single mothers may require a trusted family male influence of a grandfather, uncle or friend to take on the absent father's role.

The importance of both parents

In the last 50 years, divorce rates have skyrocketed. The tragic result is more children are being raised in single-parent homes and growing up without their father. Many couples choose to cohabit because of the painful experiences and challenges caused by the marriage breakup. Research is showing there is a higher chance of more broken relationships when couples co-habit. Life becomes very complicated for the children.

Conflicts happen in marriage and sometimes parents need counselling to resolve issues or injustices. Criticism, stonewalling, being emotionally distant or physically leaving the scene can be enormously destructive to a relationship. Life can be running at such a fast pace that your marriage and your family life could feel like you are leading to a train wreck. If that is where you are leading to, I urge you to seek professional counselling or natural therapies like kinesiology to overcome some of the stresses and challenges in your relationship.

Stop and appreciate life, make time, connect, communicate respectfully, do activities together that can bring fun and laughter back again. Remember the first love you had for each other when you met. Go through your photo albums and remember when you were courting, your wedding, and when your children came into your lives. Couples who raise issues with one another constructively, compromise and forgive one another for the wrongs done, generally have happier marriages and happier children.

Peace is not absence of conflict,
it is the ability to handle conflict by peaceful means.
Ronald Regan

It is up to you to make your marriage relationship grow and mature with love, responsibility, and commitment. Except in rare cases such as abuse or immoral behaviour, it is a better decision for couples to work out their differences, with respect and love, for the sake of the children.

There are benefits when fathers show affection to their wives on a daily basis. The loving interaction between the mother and father teaches their children to feel safe and to have respect for one another. When the parents treat each other with love and respect, and the father deals with conflicts in an appropriate and constructive manner, boys learn to understand how to treat females respectfully and are less likely to act in an aggressive manner towards females. Girls who expect men to treat them respectfully are less likely to be involved in violent or unhealthy relationships. Research has shown that parents who display anger, show contempt, or use the silent treatment are more likely to have children who are anxious, withdrawn or antisocial.

Children need both of their parents, because each parent helps a child understand masculinity and femininity. Fathers can role model honourable behaviour from a male's perspective and the mother can do so from a female's perspective. Statistics show that a father's active presence is a significant factor in helping girls avoid premature sex and pregnancy, and develop a sense of independence and self-assertiveness.

Carla Hannaford, a biologist, educator and author of *Smart Moves* says:

> *"Developmental experts agree that the only factor shown to optimise children's intellectual potential is a secure, trusting relationship with their parents or caregiver. Time spent cuddling, playing, being fully present and consciously communicating with children establishes a bond of security, trust and respect on which the entire child-development*

pyramid is based. School children must also feel safe, accepted and included in order for learning to occur."

Break the failure cycle

Bringing you and your spouse, and your entire family together, often just needs the support of a good tool. Over the years, I have found Brain Gym® to be one of the most pro-active tools a family can incorporate into their lives, with tremendous benefits to both parents and their children.

Brain training systems, like Brain Gym®, work so well because there is no standard that a child must fit into. Instead, it empowers them to use their innate abilities, and helps them to see that they can do things they previously thought too difficult. They learn to replace negative thoughts with positive affirmations, problem-solving abilities and confidence.

The brain and the body, working together in harmony, can lead to a sense of well-being and forms the basis of self-esteem. Lacking self-esteem means that the body and brain have a disconnect. It can mean that our reactions to what happens daily are conflicting or confusing. Functioning from the left side of our brain, the logic side, can cause over-analysis and viewing others and ourselves critically. Functioning mainly with the right side of our brain, however, can mean being passive, vague, or lost in our feelings, feeling victimised, and allowing others to walk all over us. This is why it is so vital that we have good self-esteem and use our entire brain together.

In children, non-integrated physiological habits can manifest themselves physically. You might see a child who must swing his leg while doing math problems, favouring one of his ears or eyes when he is reading, or even holding his breath while doing some difficult hand-eye task. In adults, it often manifests itself as visible tension or stress.

Help your child succeed

Years of experience with Brain Gym® movements, Kinesiology and Rhythmic Movement Training have taught me that people of any age can reclaim their own physical and emotional self-esteem. Brain Gym® exercises are movements that help cross the mid-lines of the body, ensuring both sides work together. By re-establishing natural learning patterns, the whole body is set on alert and eager to learn. This is the perfect state for exploring the world, testing skills and abilities, and reconnecting to their innate skills.

Fostering self-esteem is vital to the teachings of Brain Gym® exercises. Students build their self-esteem as they learn the movements and begin to use it regularly, whether at home, school, or play.

Self-esteem is shaped by:

> How a person thinks

> The person's sense of self worth

> What the person expects of himself or herself

> How other people feel and interact with him or her

In order to support the development of a child's character and self-esteem, we need to consistently point out their special gifts. They need to see how they are doing and what is special about them. Letting them know what you see about them and how special they are helps their self-esteem greatly, which in turn encourages them to work even harder.

I have always believed that a critical element of developing healthy self-esteem is being able to look beyond yourself and to the needs of others. Doing something genuinely nice for someone else always makes you feel good, as well as helps the other person. I think it is important to teach our children to do that regularly. That means thinking about how someone else may be feeling or what they may be going through. To look beyond themselves, to others and the world around them.

There are adults who struggle constantly throughout their lives because they have deep-seated feelings of inadequacy. This can result from lack of feedback or from criticism, whether physical, mental or emotional, or lack of love. Contrary to what some people think, being ignored is as bad for a person's self-esteem as being abused.

In the first years of life, three interlocking factors shape a child's self-esteem:

1. Unconditional love

2. Feelings of accomplishment for achieving goals

3. Positive encouragement from those they love most

> "Do not train a child to learn by force or harshness; but direct them to it by what amuses their minds so that you may be better able to discover with accuracy the peculiar bent of the genius of each."
>
> Plato

Tantrums – part of growing up

I have seen my fair share of tantrums with my own children growing up, especially during the time period around two to four years of age, when the emotional brain (limbic system) is being developed. I urge parents to be patient and calm as the child is learning about emotions and how to express them. During this development stage, it is the time to communicate and teach them about their feelings and emotions, and how to express them appropriately. When children are taught how to regulate their emotions, they tend to experience negative emotions for a shorter time. They also relate to people better, form stronger friendships and do better at school.

There are great books around to read to your child which talk about feelings. In her best-selling children's books, the *When I'm Feeling* series, Trace Moroney delights children and adults with eight books on *FEELINGS*. Moroney titles her books, *When I'm feeling... Jealous ... Sad ...Kind ... Angry ... Loved ... Scared ... Happy ... and Lonely.* Her delightful books will remind you why feelings are important. The books will teach your child that it is normal to feel sad, or angry, or scared at times and guide them to trust themselves in handling painful feelings and gain inner security.

Children act out for many different reasons: they are tired, they sense tension, they are bored, and they are exploring limits. Putting a stop to negative behaviour is a loving act, just as applauding a child for good efforts in school. Children need limits and boundaries, and parents need to give them the security that they will not allow the child to hurt themselves or others. Parents give children guidance in the way to act and how to be their very best. Teaching them how to respect themselves and others can make a huge difference in how they behave and treat others.

Studies have linked crime to poor self-esteem, low self-confidence, and feelings of hopelessness. Helping your child build self-esteem can go a long way towards keeping them on the straight and narrow path.

Recently, I had a client with a six-year-old daughter who was having half-hour temper tantrums every day. The mother was desperate to help her. After the first session with me, she began doing the Brain Gym® exercises and Rhythmic movement every day to integrate her reflexes. The young girl reduced her tantrums to an occasional one or two a week. Now she is able to calm herself down quickly whenever she gets upset. She has become a happier young girl and has also improved in her reading and writing. At the time of the first visit she was struggling to write two sentences and at the second session the mother was happy to report that she had written two pages that day. She had increased her capacity to communicate and express her thoughts more easily. The mother was so pleased with the results. I was really thrilled for her accomplishment.

Conflict verses Cooperation

Let's take a closer look at which habits keep conflicts going, and get in the way of cooperation. Habits like limiting time to connect with others or making labels and comparisons. There are alternative ways to eliminate the conflict produced by these habits to bring about respect and cooperation.

Language matters

How many times have you experienced an instant recognition, such as: *that sounded just like my mother or my father when they got angry?* Your habitual language of communication that you learnt as a child, can get in the way of connecting respectfully with your child. Listen to your language.

Dr. Bruce Liptons Ph.D., author of *Biology of Belief* says, *"The subconscious mind's behaviours when we are not paying attention may not be of our own creation because most of our fundamental behaviours were downloaded without question from observing other people. Because subconscious-generated behaviours are not generally observed by the conscious mind, many people are stunned to hear that they are "just like their mom or their dad," the people who programmed their subconscious minds."*

But... and Should... thinking

Using words like *but* and *should, ought* and *need,* will dramatically affect how your child will respond. Imagine your child hearing, *I really had fun at the park with you today, but...*

The word *should* communicates to your child what you expect they should be or do. Statements like: *You should be getting ready for school or You should be doing your homework now.* Your child's deep need is to be seen and heard, to be accepted and feel safe. *Should* thinking leads to blame and criticising and judgements.

When your seeing and hearing does not match the things you think things *should* be, the differences between ideal and real, emotions are triggered. The triggered emotions may provoke anger, conflict, and aggression between you and your child. Be aware of your child's needs. Why are they not getting ready for school on time? Is it because they are not feeling well? Are there any anxiety feelings caused by their teacher, school work or their class mates? Why are they not wanting to do their homework after school? They may simply need time to play and run in the backyard before settling down to do their homework, especially after being in the classroom most of the day.

Parents, in their effort to ensure compliance, find themselves commanding and demanding using phrases like *you ought to, you must,* and *you should.* Many times, children have not been given the opportunity to make their own choices to solve their own problems with your assistance. When you actively listen to your child and attempt to understand them by hearing their feelings, needs and wishes, this builds a foundation for their future relationship with you, friends and siblings.

Making comparisons

Making comparisons between your child and others can affect their self-esteem. *"Your sister is smarter than you."* Rather than encouraging your child to improve their behaviour, hurtful words will trigger jealousy, discouragement, and rebellion. Children need to be appreciated, respected, and accepted just the way they are.

Good News

You can greatly enhance your ability to connect with your children by practicing language that does not judge, criticise, blame, or demand, but instead shows a respectful awareness of your child's needs. Make a heartfelt connection with yourself and with your child to respect and care for their needs. Remember, intention is still 90 percent of communication.

We all need fun, play, learning, making choices, physical needs of fresh air, exercise, nourishing food, water, and protection, achievement, acknowledgement, creativity, knowing our gifts, appreciation by others, a belonging, sharing life's joys and sorrows, closeness, contact with nature, peace, joy, and much, much, more.

When people are in pain, they want empathy. You can listen with empathy and with respectful understanding of what your child is experiencing, putting aside judgements, opinions and fears.

Develop a habit of frequently checking in on what is going on with you, noticing feelings and needs. Notice when you are feeling negative and work on changing your feelings to a positive way. When you do this, you will find yourself more involved in doing more productive and positive actions towards yourself, your child and others.

Children will remember
the kisses, cuddles and games of peek-a-boo,
Your warmth, smell and the safety they feel when they are with you.
Most of all they will LOVE YOU, because YOU LOVE them,
That is what matters.

Anonymous

Action Plan to build your child's self-esteem

➢ **Love and trust**: Love your child unconditionally; when he's good, when he's bad, when he's happy or sad. That might sound like something Dr Seuss would write, yet it is so true. Children need to know that you love them no matter what. Tell them often how special they are and how much you love them. Find something about them to praise each day. Praise for a job well done. It teaches them that it is okay to be proud of their talents, skills, and abilities.

➢ **Teach your child diligently:** Communicate positively and connect with your child teaching them about life skills and have fun. Enjoy being with them continually whenever you are with them, travelling in the car, walking to the park, preparing meals, playing with a ball or building blocks, and eating at the dinner table. Make time, have a break, be playful with your child. Communicating face to face is becoming a lost skill as more electronic technology such as TV, computers, mobile phones, social media, and texting overtakes people lives. Praise your child regularly for their best efforts to do what is expected of them. Life gets busy and we can take them for granted when all is going well. Praise them when they need praising.

➤ **Goals**: Set easily-achievable goals for your child and their confidence will skyrocket. Have them involved in planning their goals. Teach them how to think, build on their strengths, communicate, connect, and include your message of love in all your activities together.

➤ **Praise and reward**: Give praise for anything good your child does, large or small. If they worked hard in school, tell them how proud you are. If they cleaned their room without nagging or washed the dinner dishes for you, give them lots of verbal praise. Small rewards highlight accomplishments and go a long way towards building self-esteem. Be spontaneous, *be in the moment* expressing your feelings of love to your children. Tell them, "You light up my day" or "You're my precious cutie" - whatever you feel.

➤ **Give affirmation with words, gifts or a special occasion:** Affirm that your child is loved and considered special, always. Do something special for them out of the blue, tell them always what a blessing they are to you even when they mess up. Truly believe your child is a wonderful, beautiful child God has given you. This gives them a safe haven to do things and not be afraid of failure as well as the confidence to grow and be happy.

➤ **Negative labels and finding fault**: Labelling people as an object, rather than a person, a living growing human being, can become a habit. Some parents unintentionally blurt out labels for children when they are angry or disappointed. Saying to a child *you're stupid* or *you're lazy* can affect them for life, so be very careful with your words. NEVER use the phrase, *You're a bad boy/girl.* This discourages their efforts. They may not try to do things, believing they are too stupid. This sets up the child to think they are unable to do things.

Make the child feel as if any misbehaviour on their part is inconsistent with who they are. Say, *'What you did was wrong and I can't understand why a smart, wonderful child like you would do that.'*

Identify the triggers that lead to tantrums and challenging behaviour. Look for clues to help you identify the little things that can make or break a day. Work out strategies for reducing and eliminating power struggles. Ask yourself why the child is behaving a certain way. Are their physical and emotional needs being met?

➢ **Label behaviour**: It is appropriate to tell a child when they have done something inappropriate, but it is vital to make the distinction between the behaviour being inappropriate and the child being bad. Here are a few more label words to be aware of to avoid labelling your child, such as stubborn, demanding, self-critical, wild, aggressive, disruptive, argumentative, noisy and easily bored. *Love the child and dislike the behaviour.*

➢ **Hobbies and sports:** Joining a club or sports team can help build a child's self-esteem. Find something that he or she is very interested in, whether football, ballet, karate, crafts, chess, or cooking. No matter what hobby, your child will gain new skills – they will be proud of themselves and it gives you more opportunities to praise them. Be aware that children with ADHD might decide they are bored with an activity, so have other ideas ready.

➤ **Be positive:** Always focus on the positive; have your child make a list of all the things he likes about himself - characteristics and things he can do, then post it on their wall or in the kitchen so they see it daily, and can add to it on a regular basis. Jack Canfield, world-renowned self-esteem expert, did a study in 1982 involving 100 children. He assigned them a project: to track how many positive and negative comments they received in a day. The results were astounding. Each child received an average of 460 critical or negative comments, as opposed to 75 supportive or positive comments. They heard something negative 6 times more often than something positive! Obviously, this makes it even more vital to heap tons of praise and positive encouragement on them during their formative years.

➤ **Making choices**: Choosing is spiritual in nature; it helps children develop their inherent worth by their ability to make good moral choices. Your child will mimic your beliefs and attitude you have about life. Are you grateful, patient, respectful, caring, honest, reliable, self-disciplined, courteous, kind and loving? Do you keep your promises? Are you trusting? You must be what you want your child to be. What they see you do, they believe is right.

Are you a positive guiding force in shaping your child's thoughts and moral standards? There are many people that believe that good strong conservative values can definitely help bring up happy, secure, and successful children. That is training of the mind and heart towards doing good towards oneself, God and others. A large percentage of movies today teach by example that sexual immorality, conflict, war, and the occult is okay. These negative values tend to break down family values of love, respect, trust, peace, joy, kindness, and overall physical, emotional, and mental well-being.

> ➤ **Correct firmly and gently**: Surely you have been on the end of someone's crazed rant at some point in your life. Did it make you want to do what that person wanted you to do or not! Fear could make one do it. Parents need to be firm and not out of control.

In moments of conflict there are three choices to respond:

You can decide to want to be right and get your way no matter what with angry outbursts, fighting, sulking and walking away and refusing to talk.

You can ignore it and hope it goes away and the temptation is to walk away when you don't see a way to deal with it.

You can hold the intention to connect and cooperate.

When you have the intention to connect and cooperate, you seek to understand the child's needs to find the best solution so that everyone can feel good.

> ➤ **Take a time out:** When you find yourself emotionally charged and in the battle zone with your child, and you notice you're feeling upset, afraid or angry, arguing and raising your voice, hit the pause button, and stop doing anything you will regret later. Take a deep breath, go for a walk, do yoga or Brain Gym® exercises. Connect with your feelings and needs and work out how to interact with your children with understanding and love. Teach your children to follow these steps so they can also learn to deal and resolve conflict.

➢ **Find a no-fault zone:** Be positive and supportive when your child is being irrational or abusive. When emotions are highly charged it makes good sense to delay conversation until everyone is calm and enjoying themselves again. Once you choose to have a no fault zone, a place where respect and cooperation reigns, one step at a time, a day at a time, your intentions will create a home where everyone trusts their needs will be considered and cared for. Being respectful replaces criticism, blame, and punishment. Life is more fun and wonderful for everyone.

Being a parent develops character. The key to discipline is for parents to be firm and kind, so that the child can learn cooperation and self-discipline with no loss of dignity.

Focus on encouraging your child to develop their own self-discipline by owning up to their mistakes, thinking through solutions or correcting their misdeeds, while leaving their dignity intact. Teaching self-discipline and how to handle difficult situations can help your child to grow into a responsible, resilient and resourceful adult. Developing strength, courage, patience, love, peace and joy is a virtue for all of us to strive for.

➢ **Being Respectful:** The word *respect* means *to look*. When looking at your child, you choose to focus on your child's behaviour from your point of view, desires and judgements. Maybe you could look at your child from their point of view with respect to how they are feeling and what they need.

If you focus on what's wrong with what your child did, it can sound like this: *Look what you've done! You should know better!* Connect with your child, assisting them to find a better way. Focus on their need rather than reacting to their behaviour. Connect and listen to them. For example the child has accidentally broken a glass and their lack of coordination has caused the mishap. Observe what the child was trying to do and then instruct the child how to do it in a safer way. The child can help to clean up the mess and not made to feel it is a 'punishment.'

Teaching children to be respectful of other people and their belongings is very important. Simple things like saying *please* when asking for something, saying *thank you* and being grateful when someone has done something for you, giving a seat to a senior citizen on the bus, being polite and friendly when greeting people, also keeping their bedroom tidy and putting away toys when they have finished playing with them. It takes years of consistent training for your child to follow you as a role model. Be aware and notice how you show respect.

➢ **Doing Brain Gym exercises:** Brain Gym® exercises are fun to do and help your child have better coordination and more confidence. Your child will learn how to learn faster and reason better. Physical exercise activates the mind for learning. The Brain Gym® exercises are also effective in calming the child and parent to be able to reason and change to a positive behaviour especially after a conflict.

➢ **Give gifts freely:** The best things in life are free without expectations of getting anything back. There is great joy and genuine connection with giving and receiving of gifts. The flow of the heartfelt connection is absent when there is a sense of obligation that you must give, ought to give or should give.

Think of ways you can give from the heart. Notes of appreciation for the gifts others have given to you. Explore together the gifts and talents you have been given. Make a family scrape book of events, kind deeds, artwork, drawings and happy memories. Make a list of gifts to give to others for example cookies, hand drawn cards, pot plant and photos.

For parents, appreciate the precious gift of your children. Enjoy and admire your child's laughter, liveliness and love. Admire the awe and wonder in your child's expression when they experience something new for the first time – a walk on the sand at the beach, seeing someone sing or dance, looking at fireworks, and hearing an airplane in the sky. Explore ways you and your child can become powerful givers.

By reconnecting with your natural ability to learn, and being in touch and connecting with your heart, mind and body, it is entirely possible to reclaim more self-esteem. This helps you to be in harmony with yourself and your surroundings, learn from every experience, and really know who you are, at any age. When you have a healthy self-esteem your child will model your confidence. Nurture family connections with one on one relationships and holding family get-togethers to help harmonise your family unit.

Give me patience when little hands
Tug at me ceaseless, small demands.
Give me gentle words and smiling eyes,
To keep my lips from hasty, sharp replies.
Let not fatigue, confusion or noise
Obscure my vision of life's fleeting joys
So when in years to come my house is still,
Beautiful memories its rooms may fill.
Author Unknown

 Write down the areas you would like to improve on and make a plan of action

Area to improve	Plan of Action – what, when and how
For example **Love and trust**	eg. Find something about them to praise each day. Praise for a job well done. Give hugs every morning, after school and at bedtime.
Opportunities to teach your child diligently	
Time to set goals together	
Praise and reward	
Give affirmation with words, gifts or a special occasion	
Replace words of negative labels and finding fault	

Area to improve	Plan of Action – what, when and how
Label behaviour	
Hobbies and sports	
Be positive	
Making choices	
Correct firmly and gently	
Take a time out	
Find a no-fault zone	

Area to improve	Plan of Action – what, when and how
Being Respectful	
Doing Brain Gym exercises	
Give gifts freely	

 Write your action plan ideas here.

Chapter 5

Step # 5: Give your child the skills to succeed in life

"Movement is the door to learning. To live is to move. Life is ever changing, ever shifting and ever demanding. Brain Gym® teaches us how to move with our challenges, our dreams and our goals. I believe that there are no learning disabilities, only learning blocks. We are all learning blocked to the extent that we have mastered the art of not moving."

Dr Paul Dennison, Originator of Brain Gym®

You do not need me to tell you that our world is changing rapidly. In the past two decades alone, the way we live and the way we work has been transformed by technological advancements, global business models, environmental concerns, shifting political and economic landscapes, and evolving beliefs and value systems. Consider all the types of work that exist now, that you never imagined when you were in school, and all those career paths that have since disappeared.

The reality is that no one can map out a career path for their lifetime, simply because we cannot know what types of work will exist in ten or even five years' time. Recent statistics show workers change jobs every two to three years on average. The idea of a job for life died many years ago and the rate of job turnover is only increasing with younger generations.

Preparing for an uncertain future

If we don't know what jobs will be available, then how do we equip our children with the skills they need to succeed?

In his widely acclaimed book, *A Whole New Mind*, Daniel H. Pink suggests that in an increasingly competitive market, businesses will be looking for a new type of worker. He describes this worker in terms of their brain function – referring to the qualities that emerge from the left and right hemispheres of the brain.

> ➤ **Left brainers** are logical, detail focussed, emotionally controlled, systematic, into techniques, time conscious, pattern seekers.

> ➤ **Right brainers** are intuitive, big picture focussed, spontaneous, imaginative, into rhythm and application, relationship conscious, flow seekers.

Traditionally, those displaying analytical, knowledge-based left brain qualities have been most valued in science and business, whilst those with more intuitive, creative right brain qualities were considered best suited to the arts.

I believe in the future the workplace will be looking for whole brain thinkers. Being able to utilise the whole brain becoming more adaptable and flexible to new environments.

Is the education system giving your child the skills they need to succeed?

There is a broad debate under way about the effectiveness of our educational system in preparing our children to meet the challenges of the future. Some of the common factors raised in the course of this debate include:

- ➢ Better learning programs

- ➢ Better teaching

- ➢ Better resources

- ➢ Better testing methods

- ➢ Better learning styles

However, we often fail to consider more fundamental factors that contribute to our child's success at school – their readiness to learn. There are a series of foundational skills that are necessary before a child is ready to learn, which I will describe in more detail shortly. When these foundational skills are in place, your child will be able to activate whole brain thinking. They will thrive within the educational system and, importantly, be empowered to extend their learning process beyond the classroom to continually seek their full potential as inventive, curious, collaborative explorers.

> *"The problems many children have are actually generated by too much time spent in environments in which children are expected to "behave", when a restricted environment isn't balanced out by an hour or more a day when children can run hard, laugh hard, wrestle, be daring, and engage in spontaneous play, the strain shows in their behaviour."*
>
> Patty Wipfler

Understanding the foundational learning skills

Neuroscience has shown that the development of the brain, from when we are babies, relies on interaction with the surrounding environment through our senses and through movement. The richer our experience, the more new nerve cells and neural connections are formed, and these are the superhighways for intellectual and physical performance.

In my experience of introducing Brain Gym® to countless families, I have found that learning disabilities often arise because children have not been given the time or support they need to develop their foundational learning skills. These foundational skills encompass the very first stage of brain development, including the reflexes, sensory development, and perception motor development. Brain Gym® teaches these skills and thereby activates whole brain thinking.

The first stage of brain development is the reflexes. The primitive reflexes are automatic, stereotyped movements that ensure survival in the first weeks of life. An example is the rooting reflex which triggers an open mouth response when baby is hungry and touched by another person – it helps baby to feed. These reflexes are driven by the central nervous system (primitive brain) and are later inhibited by the frontal lobes (thinking brain) as a part of normal development. The postural reflexes develop next and are related to posture, movement, and stability.

Problems with this development process, such as prolonged primitive reflex activity beyond six to twelve months or delayed maturity of postural reflexes, can impede development in other areas. For example, crawling is one of the early building blocks for learning as it promotes gross and fine motor control, integrates the senses (second stage of development), and grows neural pathways. When basic skills such as crawling have not been successfully automated, this can limit a child's ability to take in information and learn, despite the acquisition of later skills.

Sometimes the reflexes have to be stimulated to activate them. I would like to share this miraculous experience I had with a baby many years ago.

"The baby was born through an emergency caesarean. When I went to visit her eighteen hours after the birth, her mum was concerned about her breast feeding. The baby had no desire to suck even with the encouragement of her mother. The mother and I thought about what we could do to encourage the baby to suck. The baby did not go through the birth canal to stimulate the senses and reflexes because of the emergency caesarean. I decided to massage the baby from her head to her toes. I used a very firm, tight, gentle massage to imitate the birth process to stimulate the senses. After the massage, we placed the baby on the mother's stomach. The next thing we saw was the baby crawl to the breast and start sucking. The sucking reflex and the crawling reflex was activated. It was miraculous to see it happening before our eyes!"

There are 3 stages of development

Vision, hearing, gross fine motor coordination, eye hand coordination, body awareness, being able to cross the midline is what develops through reflexes, sensory and motor development.

Reflexes - 1st Stage

Motor development during the first three years depends on the child interacting with the environment and progressing through a series of reflexes

➢   Primitive reflexes   ➢   Postural reflexes

Development of the sensory system - 2nd Stage

Each has a sense organ through which information is gained. They depend upon each other for interpretation of information and movement. Each sensory system has its own neurological network, pathway, and location within the brain.

➢ Vision   ➢ Hearing   ➢ Smell   ➢ Taste   ➢ Touch/tactile

➢ Vestibular system   ➢ Proprioceptive / kinaesthetic System

Perceptual Motor Development - 3rd Stage

The development of complex motor skills depends upon the nervous system's growth, a process called readiness, maturity, or developmental level. Growth or a change in the nervous system must precede the development of new movement or motor skills.

It involves the ability of the brain to receive, organise, interpret, and use the vast amount of sensory information that enters the body and neurological system through both external and internal stimuli. After receiving this information from each of the senses, movement of the body and gravity it must be integrated and interpreted before children can successfully function in the world around them.

➤ Gross / fine motor coordination ➤ Eye hand coordination

➤ Body awareness ➤ Laterality integration

➤ Directionality hemispheres ➤ Midline

➤ Left/right dominance ➤ Visual perception

➤ Language skills ➤ Auditory perception

➤ Ability to shut out distractions

It is important to understand each stage of development and ensure that these skills have been successfully integrated to enable whole brain learning. This will give your child the skills they need to succeed in the classroom and, more importantly, the ability to engage in the lifelong learning necessary to thrive in a changing world.

The reflexes and postural reflexes

The baby's brain certainly has not matured. For proper brain functioning, all of a person's neural connections must develop. Properly developed nerve fibres are coated with insulating myelin, and the foundation for this growth is critical throughout the first years of life. In fact, estimates are that newborn babies develop 4.7

million nerve cell branches in their brain every single minute of the first year of life.

This process is highly dependent on outside stimulation of all the infant's senses to develop adequately. Especially crucial during this period is stimulation of the tactile, balance, and kinaesthetic senses. A baby gets these stimulations by being touched and rocked, and by making continuous rhythmic movements of their own. Most babies follow a similar pattern of development - turning over, rolling, creeping along on their stomachs, rocking on their hands and knees, and then crawling - all important parts of normal development. All of these things taken together stimulate the baby's brain during the first year and are the foundation for all future development, and the maturation of the child's brain.

Children without adequate stimulation of these types can have delays in brain maturity or obvious impairments. This delayed development can manifest itself as attention disorder, with or without the related hyperactivity. When babies are unable, or not permitted, to move around sufficiently, they get insufficient stimulation of the neocortex and frontal lobes of the brain. Indications typically show up as sluggishness, hypo-activity, inattention, and late developing.

The developmental stages of an infant

Let's look at a few examples on how to recognise a reflex, whether the reflex is still retained and not integrated by a certain time, and how it will affect a child or adult in their movement and learning.

In order to survive, an infant is equipped with primitive reflexes designed to ensure immediate response to its new environment. Primitive reflexes are automatic, stereotyped movements directed by the brain stem. They are essential for the child's survival for the first few weeks of the infant's life. The primitive reflexes emerge in utero, are present at birth, and should be inhibited by six months to twelve months of age at the latest. Prolonged primitive reflex activity may prevent the development of the succeeding postural reflexes. If the primitive reflexes are retained, it is evidence of structural weakness or immaturity of the central nervous system.

Through my research and study, I have learnt that the stages of child development lay the foundation for accurate intentional movements and setting up of the internal wiring of the brain. Once the movement is integrated, we are able to perform the movement easily. If this does not occur the child will find it difficult to read, write, focus, concentrate, and sit still. It's as one parent described it: like "having an infant still active within a seven year old child".

The vestibular system is a special sensory apparatus in our inner ear. This body balance mechanism helps us to know where up is, so we can maintain equilibrium. Effective vestibular training from whole body movements like hopping, skipping, rolling, dancing, tumbling, running, and slow cross-crawling movements will assist in its development. A child with vestibular difficulties can't sit still. They tend to lose balance more easily and have more playground accidents. They move in order to know where they are in space. The vestibular is activated whenever the body and head moves and helps to relate to gravity.

The vestibular is connected to the Reticular Activating System. If there is a weakness in the system, information will not go to the senses, and then on to the cortex, the thinking part of the brain. The vestibular system is being stimulated when a child hops, skips and jumps. A child who can't sit still instinctively knows they need to get moving to acquire balance. Stillness is the most advanced level of the vestibular development. Children who are not able to stand on one leg may indicate that the vestibular system is not functioning adequately. Many adults have that challenge, which can be improved with Brain Gym® and Rhythmic Movement Training.

> Childhood is like building
> with blocks
> Each new layer of
> development builds on the last
> and it's heaps of fun

Basic Movement Development Patterns and Underlying Reflexes

The basic movement development patterns and underlying reflexes are:

➤ Breathing – Fear, Paralysis and Moro

➤ Navel Radiation

➤ Mouthing – Rooting, Sucking and Swallowing

➤ Spinal Movement – Oral Rooting, Neck Mobility, Tonic Labyrinthine, Labyrinthine Head Righting Galant, - Abdominal and Anal Rooting

➤ Homologous – Babkin, Moro, Symmetrical Tonic Neck, Inclined Symmetrical Tonic Neck

➤ Homolateral – Asymmetrical Tonic Neck and Hand to Mouth

➤ Contralateral – Tonic Lumber and Lumbar Reach

(Adapted from *Sensing, Feeling, and Action*, by Bonnie Bainbridge Cohen and *A Teacher's Window Into a Child's Mind*, by Sally Goddard, 1997)

How to recognise a retained reflex

Each infant reflex movement is triggered by a sound, touch, and change of position. When the reflex is triggered it causes an involuntary movement. It is said to be retained. Children, teens and adults who can't sit still have retained reflexes still present in the body.

Root and Suck Reflex

When an infant's cheek is touched the mouth moves towards the hand or nipple. It is present at birth and integrated by four months. If this reflex is retained, the child may have a hard time articulating words (for example saying wed instead of red), and may chew or bite objects. The infant is oversensitive to touch on his cheek or mouth and may have difficulty taking in nourishment, seemingly being a fussy eater.

Moro Reflex

When an infant hears a sudden sound, he will throw his arms out and take in a quick gasp of air and slowly draw his arms back in towards his body. This reflex should integrate at two to four months. When retained, the child may overreact to fears and startles at nearly every sudden sound. When the Moro is activated the defence mechanisms of the body are on alert and hormones are secreted, the body experiences sensitivities. They may suffer sensitivity to foods, adrenal fatigue leading to allergy, asthma or chronic illness and emotional ups and downs. When an infant's moro reflex is triggered, they will cry and the mother will run to hug and rock the baby. This will help integrate the moro reflex so the child will calm down and feel safe. Otherwise the baby will not feel safe.

Fear Paralysis

The infant has a tendency to retreat from anything threatening. This is to be integrated by the time of birth. The fear paralysis reflex can still be retained in adults who have been raised up in a stressful environment. A child with a retained paralysis would be extremely shy, anxious, tendency to motion sickness, panic attacks, phobias and avoid eye contact.

From fear paralysis to a happier adventurous child

"I am a mother of a three-year-old daughter. I have had severe challenges with her since six months of age. She was a very scared child. She could not be placed in the pram or car as she would always scream being separated from me. We went to several therapist for one and half years. I was informed she had fear paralysis and that no one could help her. She was a child that when we went to the playground she would sit on me and scream as she didn't feel comfortable being with other people. She never left my side. This became very challenging when I became pregnant with my second child. I was desperate and I started going online searching for help and Enza's name came up with Brain Gym® and Rhythmic Movement Training. I vividly remember the day when I asked for help and made an appointment.

By six sessions, my daughter has made tremendous changes. Now I have a daughter who is adventurous, she climbs up everything and is doing things beyond her age. She is better with people and no longer screams to sit on me. She is better at communicating to me when she is frightened. For the last two years, she would scream when we washed her hair. Two months ago, she started washing her own hair and enjoys it. In the last two years, we couldn't stop her biting her nails and now she no longer bites her nails. There is still more to do before she starts kindergarten. Yet, seeing all these changes happening every time we saw Enza was very exciting for us. Enza has helped us a lot and we are very thankful."

Sabine, Mother

Palmar Reflex or Grasp Reflex

A touch on the inside of the infants hand causes him to grip very hard and may cause mouth or tongue to move when manipulating objects; for example, an open mouth response when catching a ball. Independent movement of fingers will tend to weaken other muscles of the body. This reflex is normally integrated by two to three months. If not, it will show in a child having poor manual dexterity, such as holding a pencil in a tense fist-like grip or moving the tongue and mouth while writing.

Spinal Galant Reflex

A touch on the infant's side near the waist triggers a pulling away movement. This reflex normally integrates by three to nine months. A child with this retained reflex can't sit still, is easily tickled, doesn't rest against his chair, dislikes elastic waistbands and tight clothing and wet or soil themselves.

Tonic Labyrinthine Reflex (TLR)

TLR involves the vestibular system which provides a sense of balance and works out your posture in space. Forward movement of head causes the infant's arms and legs to bend, while backward movement causes the arms and legs to extend. This reflex normally integrates by four months. If this reflex is retained, some children will have low muscle tone or will slouch and prop up the head on his hand while writing. He will struggle with sequencing, organisation skills, short term memory and have difficulty focusing near and far. It can be also associated with motion sickness, poor balance, and difficulty judging space, distance, depth and speed.

Asymmetrical Tonic Neck Reflex (ATNR)

When the infant turns his head, his arm and legs extend and follow while opposite side draws into the body. This reflex should be integrated by six months. If this reflex is retained, a child will struggle to concentrate, tying shoes, balancing, and ball catching. This reflex helps make connection between touch, sight and vision and establishes distance perception and hand-eye coordination.

Symmetrical Tonic Neck Reflex (STNR)

Backward movement of the head causes the arms to straighten, hip and legs to bend. This reflex is normally integrated by nine to eleven months. A child with retained STNR would have difficulty focusing in the classroom, wriggling in his chair, and does not want to stay on his chair. Poor posture and coordination is due to low muscle tone.

Here is a wonderful testimonial from a very diligent mother and son who first came to see me 6 months ago.

Remarkable rehabilitation from paraplegia to taking a few steps in 6 months

"In 2009, at the age of 2, our son was diagnosed with a spinal cancer. The tumour was enclosed within the spinal canal, squashing his nerves against the bone causing paraplegia. Following his surgery to remove the tumour and free his nerve cells, our son remained paralysed. He had lost all muscular and nerve function from the waist down. Yet, from out of all this heart ache, there came a little

---

ray of light. We were told our son may remain a paraplegic, his nerves may regenerate themselves due to his age or his nerves may reconnect. With this knowledge in our mind, spirit and heart, we endeavoured to give our son every fighting chance to regain normal function.

Weekly physio and monthly massage therapy, our son adapted to his new life in his wheelchair. His upper body strength continued to thrive, as they taught him the ins and outs of using his wheelchair. A TLSO (turtle shell) was made for him to wear daily to help straighten his spinal cord. Our son wore the shell unwillingly for two months, after that he refused to wear the shell. With the focus of our son's rehabilitation on his upper body and safety in his wheelchair, there was little improvement in his lower limbs. We started to look for a therapist who would embrace our son, work with him holistically and work with his lower limbs.

At six years of age, we took our son to see Enza Lyons, we wanted to know if there was any way in which we could retrain his brain to encourage movement and functioning of his lower limbs. At our first appointment our son's movement was very limited. His left leg and foot was limp, with no movement or sensation. His right foot was limp but his leg had involuntary muscle contraction. His core muscles were weak with a 60% lumber lordosis.

Enza worked with our son once a month. At home, we followed on with the Brain Gym® Exercises, Rhythmic Movements, PACE and balloon play.

After seven sessions with Enza, the improvement in our son's physical and sensory function is remarkable. He has controlled voluntary movement in this left and right leg. He can crawl on his hands and knees, pull himself up on furniture to stand and furniture walk for small distances. His 60% lumber lordosis has decreased to 40% as a result of his core strengthening. He is more aware of his body and the capabilities of his lower limbs. He has regained a degree of pelvic and limb sensation.

We are all thrilled at his accomplishment as he continues rehabilitation. He has achieved all this in the last 6 months.

Holistically, he has become a more confident and capable young man, believing in himself to make good choices which are beneficial to himself and the world."

Kerry, Mother

Action Plan to solve retained reflexes

In order to resolve these issues with retained reflexes, Educational Kinesiology, which Brain Gym® is a part of, and Rhythmic Movement Training, and other motor sensory therapies, can effectively integrate the reflexes. It does not need to be a lengthy session. Some reflexes are mildly retained and children can respond quickly using the simple five-step re-patterning balance process. Children enjoy doing the movements. These programs are very successful in integrating the reflexes allowing the child to improve learning, coordination, and behaviour.

It is important to understand each stage of development and ensure that these skills have been successfully integrated to enable whole brain learning. The reflexes are the foundation for each stage of development to build upon. This will give your child the skills they need to succeed in the classroom and, more importantly, the ability to engage in the lifelong learning necessary to thrive in a changing world.

The human body has an amazing ability to heal. Miracles do happen and past diagnoses can become obsolete. Be ready to take your child out of a labelled box and develop the potential genius in your child.

 Write your action plan ideas here.

CHAPTER 6

Step # 6: Use music to enhance learning and confidence

"Music is shown to be a strong developer of emotions, even before birth. Newborns are able to recognise the music their mothers listened to during pregnancy . . . The earlier children are introduced to music, via listening, singing, exploring musical instruments and dancing, the more their brains develop and the more able they are to feel and responsibly express emotions in a healthy way."

Carla Hannaford, author of Smart Moves

Music For Learning

Extensive research has demonstrated the power of music as a natural therapy for learning, improved health and well-being, and high performance.

If your child is exposed to a wide variety of music from an early age – including baroque, classical, and romantic eras, and with singing from a wide variety of cultures, the child also has the best chance of developing a good level of musical intelligence.

The ability to develop listening skills is also a key part of learning, and both listening and musical abilities are closely linked with your child's development.

How music can help children

The power of music can be applied in many areas, but most importantly for our purposes, it can assist with overcoming developmental and learning disabilities by helping children with:

➢ speech, language and communication

➢ anxiety and stress relief

➢ socialisation

➢ physical and motor skills

➢ motivation

➢ cognitive function

➢ concentration

➢ ability to cope and emotional balance

Using music to enhance the benefits of the Brain Gym® program

Brain Gym® uses specific exercises and movements to activate neural connections in our brain (the superhighways for intellectual and physical development) to optimise brain function and to stimulate the learning process.

The targeted use of music alongside Brain Gym® greatly enhances the process.

Singing, playing musical instruments, and dancing all encourage movement, integration of mind and body, and sensory stimulation – key elements of the Brain Gym® system. These activities also increase children's confidence and self-esteem, provide a release for creative energy, and improve physical co-ordination.

Studies have shown that schools with high quality music and arts programs generally have more academically successful students. Also, after taking up a musical instrument, students usually achieve better grades.

Quick tips for parents

Learning is closely linked to movement. Bounce your baby on your knees as you sing to him or her. Dance with your young child, sing with them, clap your hands. Singing helps with language, rhythm, and memory development. Encourage your child to play a musical instrument. Use music for relaxation – Vivaldi's, The Four Seasons, or almost any work of Mozart. Expose them to quality music. Children enjoy movement, dancing and singing.

Impressed with results!

"I would recommend that all staff use it as a whole school approach to overcoming learning difficulties. I would estimate the increased productivity to be 400 percent compared to teaching without Brain Gym®. When teaching music, I could teach in depth, in a half hour lesson, 8 lines of music with Brain Gym® compared to 2 lines per half hour without it. In spelling, Brain Gym® before every session for one term, once a week, resulted in accuracy going from 2 out of 20 to 20 out of 20! Imagine the self-esteem, the feeling of achievement those students experienced. This was far more rewarding than any other behaviour strategy that I have found so far."

Sandra, Teacher

Quick tips for using Brain Gym® and music in the classroom

Another way that music can be used to enhance the Brain Gym® and learning process is to use it as a background accompaniment. When used before, during and after learning experiences, music and Brain Gym® together enable children to be more receptive to the process and receive maximum benefit.

When using music in the classroom to enhance learning:

> ➤ instrumental music is best as voices and lyrics can be distracting

> ➤ use marching beat music with Brain Gym® to activate mind-body connection before learning

> ➤ use Mozart for focused work such as writing, maths, creative problem-solving and reasoning

> ➤ use nature sound-scapes with limited instrumentals to encourage deeper states of relaxed reflection and creativity

Music counteracting electromagnetic fields

I recently came across some interesting information about music that I thought was important to share.

It is a well-known fact that our world is polluted with electromagnetic fields, and that these areas can affect our health and well-being.

According to the United States' National Aeronautic and Space Administration (NASA), there is a way we can neutralise the effects of those fields. They have done studies which prove that eliminating those factors which decrease our coordination, balance, strength, and flexibility can be done by listening to certain pieces of music. Internationally known guitarist, Mark Romero's music has been studied by NASA and shown incredible results in counteracting electromagnetic fields.

I am excited to be sharing this revolutionary approach for creating higher levels of heath, well-being, and consciousness.

Mark Romero states, "In our modern-day world, we have virtually surrounded ourselves with over 80,000 man-made chemicals that have permeated into our air, food, and water. Virtually every aspect of our lives has been touched by these impurities.

In addition to these chemicals, we have also surrounded ourselves with a vast amount of electronic technology that is producing electromagnetic fields (EMFs) that are causing stress and compromising our quality of life.

Quantum physics has redefined the world we live in. Where before we thought we were solid bone and muscle, we now realize that we are expressions of a field of energy, and we are learning that these negative influences are interrupting our energy, causing stress, compromising our health and lowering levels of consciousness.

A few years ago, a former top consultant to NASA discovered frequencies in my music that actually null-and-void the negative effects of these interrupters, opening the door to dramatic reductions of stress, improved physical energy, more vitality, and higher levels of consciousness. You have the opportunity to experience for yourself the power of the music".

Specific music can help shield us and our children, and re-tune our energy with vibrations of certain tones in music. In fact, within ten minutes, music can relieve stress and put you into a deep sleep. Additionally, you will notice a calming effect and increased focus when playing music like Mozart in the background. This type of sound therapy when used with positive affirmations, music, and visualisation can help free people from limiting thoughts, perceptions, and beliefs that are holding them back.

Action Plan to Enhance Learning with Music

➢ Listen to a variety of music from different countries

➢ Move, dance, clap and sing to music

➢ Play background music

➢ Investigating musical instruments

> Explore what feeling the piece of music gives you

> Encourage your child to listen to positive uplifting music, assist them to understand and teach them how music can also make you feel depressed and down and to choose the songs that make one feel happy

> Conduct to music

> Draw to music

> Be creative and make your own song together

> Make home-made music using glass bottles filled with water

> Use home-made instruments to play with classical music in the background

> Develop a love for quality music

> Take lessons and learn to play an instrument or two

> Get your child involved with a music program at school

Write your action plan ideas here.

CHAPTER 7

Step # 7: Reduce stress and empower your child to become calmer, happier, and successful

"Childhood is not a race to see how quickly a child can read, write and count.
Childhood is a small window of time to learn and develop at the pace which is right for each individual child.
Your child is where they are, because they need to be.
No amount of pressure will make them learn any faster, yet will only serve to destroy their confidence.
Replace pressure and frustration with patience, love and support and your child will grow into a happy well-adjusted adult."

Author Unknown

The hidden danger sabotaging your child's learning

There are many factors that may contribute to your child experiencing poor concentration and early learning difficulties, moodiness, inappropriate behaviour - and stress is one that is often overlooked.

We like to think of childhood as a time of carefree play, unburdened by adult responsibilities. However, in our modern, fast-paced society, our every activity from a very young age is scheduled, scrutinised, and measured. Whether it's achieving better grades, winning the grand finale, or having lots of friends, there are many situations in which children feel pressure to perform.

Moreover, when we are so frequently stressed by our own relationships, finances, and careers (just to name a few common concerns), why would we then think that children are immune to this influence?

In fact, stress and anxiety are real problems for children and can certainly contribute to serious early learning difficulties or delayed development of important educational skills, such as learning to read and write. It can also impact on children's long-term health and well-being.

How does stress and anxiety sabotage your child's learning?

As an adult in our fast-paced society, we are all too aware of the effects stress can have on us. Inability to focus on the task at hand and feelings of helplessness, sensitivities to criticism, depression, paranoia, and resentment can all result from stresses placed on us as adults. Additionally, we might have trouble remembering things we know and processing new information, or become easily distracted and prone to mistakes. What we fail to realise sometimes is that stress is just as harmful to our children.

> *"Stress is a reaction of perceived threat. The stress response prepares the individual to mentally and physically take protective action. . . . But the stress response does not make us smart, creative or rational."*
>
> Carla Hannaford Ph.D. (Neurobiologist)

Stress effects can also cause learning difficulties. Your child's ability to learn is directly impacted when they are under stress, because the stress response:

> ➤ decreases blood flow to the higher areas of the brain that have to do with planning, memory, insight and learning

> ➤ increases muscle tension throughout the body which can lead to chronic pain and digestive problems

> ➤ increases heart rate to distribute oxygen around the body, thereby reducing oxygen available to the brain

> ➤ dilutes pupils to increase peripheral vision and heighten awareness of potential danger, thereby reducing reading abilities

> ➤ induces hypersensitivity to sound to heighten awareness of potential danger, thereby reducing ability to concentrate on instructions and take reasoned action.

Does your child display the danger signs of stress and anxiety?

> ➤ Does your child complain about headaches and pains in the neck, shoulders or jaw?

> ➤ Does your child have bad dreams or wet the bed?

> ➤ Does your child have difficulty adapting to change and do they question what will happen in the future?

> ➤ Does your child have difficulty understanding instructions and often appears distracted?

> ➤ Does your child suffer from moodiness or emotional outbursts?

> ➤ Does your child do letter or number reversals, for example writing b's instead of d's?

The 7 learning blocks to your child's success

If your child is struggling with one or more of the 7 learning blocks to success, it critically undermines their ability to develop intellectually, emotionally and physically.

Do you recognise one or more of these seven learning blocks to success affecting your child?

1. **Poor concentration:** Your child is unable to settle, is easily distracted, is constantly fidgeting and puts off tasks for a later time.

2. **Reading difficulties:** Your child reads slowly, stumbles over words, lacks comprehension or expresses a reluctance to read.

3. **Inability to relate to others or express feelings:** Your child is disruptive in class, is often moody or angry, has few friends and can be inconsiderate of others. They don't like to talk about their feelings.

4. **Anxiety:** Your child worries constantly about tests, tensions in the home or "what if?" scenarios. They do not adapt well to change and may occasionally wet the bed.

5. **Low self-esteem:** Your child frequently expresses negative views about themselves, is reluctant to socialise with others, has difficulty making choices like what to wear, and is generally unhappy.

6. **Poor coordination:** Your child is clumsy when catching balls or handling household items, confuses left and right, has difficulty holding a pencil, and may feel dizzy when playing sports.

7. **Frequent stress-related illness:** Your child has a poor appetite, suffers from stomach aches before going to school, experiences frequent colds, ear infections and headaches, grinds teeth at night, suffers from a sore jaw or has poor posture.

Sometimes these learning blocks are diagnosed as learning or attention disorders, such as ADD or ADHD, Dyslexia, Dyspraxia, Autism, or Asperger's Syndrome. Sometimes there is no formal diagnosis, yet otherwise intelligent children are labelled 'slow developers' or 'under achievers'. This is not only demoralising for your child, it also increases the stress in your home and can impact on your relationships, your work and your health.

If your child is struggling with one or more of the 7 learning blocks to success, Brain Gym® is one solution that has made the difference for many children. In my practice, doing personal one-on-one sessions, I combined several motor sensory programs together to bring on faster results to overcome these learning blocks.

Brain Gym® is a safe, drug free, learning program that uses a range of dynamic movements and techniques to support the development of key, sensorimotor abilities – readiness skills – that make learning easier and more pleasurable. While any physical exercises may 'wake up' the brain, the 26 Brain Gym® activities further foster the flexibility, eye teaming, and hand-eye coordination that allow learners to thrive in the classroom, along with the ability to live happily and creatively amid the stressors of modern life.

A great help to my students and my own daughter

"I use Brain Gym® with my students and it greatly improved their concentration and focus on their lessons. On a personal level, the greatest success I've had is with my own daughter. A reluctant reader and a quiet student, Brain Gym® has been instrumental in greatly increasing her self-confidence. She has improved in all academic areas and is a happier child. I strongly recommend Brain Gym® to all."

Joanne, Teacher

More Focused, Consistent & Positive

"I am more focused, consistent and positive. Doing the Brain Gym® exercises takes no time at all and there is an immediate positive affect – practical tool I can use any time I feel the need... Thank you, Enza."

Peta, Teacher

Settles down stressed and angry students

"In my class of children aged five to seven, many students were unsettled, stressed and angry. Consequently, many were experiencing learning difficulties and displaying very challenging and disruptive behaviour.

After introducing daily Brain Gym® exercises, the results have been amazing. Many of the parents have commented how their children are progressing in many different areas including coordination, balance and confidence. Parents are telling me that their children are much happier and will even do the Brain Gym® exercises at home to help themselves to relax and cope with challenging situations.

One particular grade two student was experiencing difficulties with her reading and writing, was putting a lot of pressure on herself, was often very tired, and was finding it difficult to relax. After three or four sessions with Enza, this student's reading and writing improved greatly and she has greater confidence in herself. She has transformed from a little girl who was often upset by the 'smallest things', to a happy child who is so much more energetic and confident in herself and her abilities.

Brain Gym® is a simple, but very powerful 'tool', and it can really make a difference in children's lives. I would highly recommend it to other teachers and parents."

Sandra, Primary School Teacher

Deactivating the stress response for successful learning

It is clear that stress and anxiety can be key contributors to children's early learning difficulties or to other developmental problems they may experience with socialisation, literacy, and physical co-ordination.

The effects of stress can be easily overcome by movement, such as by:

➢ Relieving body tension and relaxing the body

➢ Strengthening communication between the brain and body

➢ Improving breathing and adding oxygen to the brain

➢ Reducing stress-inducing chemicals and increasing 'feel good' chemicals

➢ Strengthening pathways linking both sides of the brain

Using movement and exercise to reduce stress improves the brain's capacity to think imaginatively, create goals, and focus on meeting them. Listening to soothing music can change our brain's response as well.

For this reason, Brain Gym® incorporates techniques that empower children to:

➢ work through whatever anxieties or fears are holding them back

➢ gain confidence with fun, easy exercises

➢ engage higher reasoning to overcome any problem or stressful situation

➢ activate the mind-body connection to regain a calm, relaxed focus

For your child's success, be aware of how stress is affecting them and consider ways you can empower them to become calmer and happier every day.

Ideal learning today emphases relaxation with movement; this keeps the student in the proper state to absorb the most learning possible.

I am
I am not built to sit still
keep my hands to myself, take turns,
be patient, stand in line, or keep quiet.
I need motion, I need novelty,
I need adventure, and
I need to engage the world with my whole body.
Let me PLAY!
(Trust me, I'm learning)
Author unknown

Brain Gym® and how it works

Brain Gym® is the result of over 30 years of development by Paul E Dennison, Ph.D. and Gail E Dennison, pioneers in applied brain research.

It is now taught across more than 80 countries in schools, corporations, performing arts programs and sports centres. The success of these techniques has been proven in clinical experience, field studies and published reports. Now, the latest scientific research shows us how it works.

The discovery of neuroplasticity, hailed as one of the most important scientific breakthroughs of the 20th century, has proven that the brain can re-wire itself throughout our lives in response to thinking, learning and **movement**. In fact, all learning, from the time we are babies, involves movement.

As we grow, we move and learn and the brain forms new nerve cells and neural connections – the superhighways for intellectual and physical performance.

In his best-selling book, *The Brain That Changes Itself,* Dr Norman Doidge, Psychiatrist, Psychoanalyst and researcher, describes his investigation of neuroplasticity and reports that:

> *". . . children are not always stuck with the mental abilities they are born with . . . I met people whose learning disorders were cured and whose IQs were raised; I saw evidence that it is possible for eighty-year-olds to sharpen their memories to function the way they did when they were fifty-five."*

Balanced Brain, Balanced Body

Brain Gym® uses easy and enjoyable exercises that take only 15 minutes a day to enhance our left and right brain function. Each side of the body is controlled by the opposite brain hemisphere. As we move opposite arms and legs through the targeted Brain Gym® movements, we activate whole brain function and enhance learning and behaviour.

Brain Gym® puts your child in charge of their own success and they love it!

> ➤ With Brain Gym®, they can feel the difference almost immediately and this gives them confidence.

> ➤ With Brain Gym®, they get better grades, perform better in sports and the arts, and relate better to friends and family.

Imagine your child....

> ➤ relaxed and able to concentrate in school

> ➤ confident that they can do their best in any situation – whether learning, creating, or playing sport

> ➤ happy, relating well to others, and not overwhelmed by negative emotions

> ➤ empowered to follow their own path to personal success and fulfilment.

Brain Gym® can help you too!

Not only will you experience the joy of watching your child become happier, healthier, more relaxed and more confident, you can also learn to use Brain Gym® to improve your own physical mental and emotional well-being. Brain Gym® is a safe, natural physical therapy that can help the whole family with stress relief, workplace performance, health problems, anxiety, depression and relationships.

Here is a recent testimonial from a grateful parent who reduced her stress levels.

"I have experienced stress-related depression, panic and anxiety attacks, poor concentration, memory problems, mood changes, and hormonal problems over a number of years. After an initial appointment with Enza, I feel much more relaxed, and more able to face new challenges and experiences. I encourage others to seek out this pleasant and enjoyable program. Thank you Enza."

Rose Ann

Learning more about Brain Gym® movements

The 26 Brain Gym® activities support the development of key sensorimotor abilities that make learning easier and more pleasurable. Brain Gym® is a fun learning program that assists in all stages of child development, language development, coordination, gross motor skills and fine motor skills, stress relief, creativity, and problem-solving skills. There are a variety of books available that describe the Brain Gym® movements and their benefits, as listed in Chapter 9 under Books and Resources.

You may also choose to visit and learn from a licensed Brain Gym® instructor/consultant in your area. In a private session, they will show you how to use the Brain Gym® more effectively and assist you and your child's specific needs.

This is how personal one-on-one sessions can make a difference.

> *"I now bring Oliver to see Enza to do Brain Gym® and Rhythmic Movement. Last year we had a horrible year at school. It was very difficult. Oliver was not able to sit still. He was not following instructions. He was in trouble every day from the teachers and from other parents. We discovered Brain Gym® and we have been coming along to see Enza.*
>
> *Oliver's school life now is so much better. He is one of the top readers in his class. Socially he is making connections with friends. The other parents are happy and smiling at me rather than rousing at me. We are so happy that we have found Brain Gym®. It's been fantastic for us."*
>
> Amanda, Mother

By attending the Brain Gym® 101 course, you will learn all of the movements and how to use them effectively with the 5-step balance process to achieve greater success and improvements in your child's learning, concentration, reading, writing, organisation, coordination, behaviour, and much more. At the course you will learn hands on practical applications in applying Brain Gym® movements in your everyday life.

> *"This Brain Gym® Professional Development Program has been fantastic. I have an 8-month old daughter, a wife, and I am a PE teacher. I see something for everybody. I thoroughly recommend the Brain Gym® program. It's been one of the best Professional Development program I have ever been too. Thank you very much."*
> Craig, PE Teacher

 Write your action plan ideas here.

CHAPTER 8

Conclusion

Qualities to build in your child

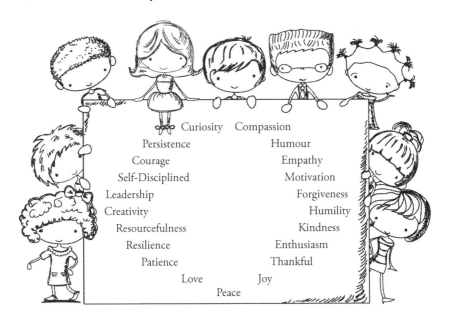

Curiosity	Compassion
Persistence	Humour
Courage	Empathy
Self-Disciplined	Motivation
Leadership	Forgiveness
Creativity	Humility
Resourcefulness	Kindness
Resilience	Enthusiasm
Patience	Thankful
Love	Joy
Peace	

These qualities not measured by school tests

Raising a happy, healthy, and well-adjusted child is challenging, especially in the fast-paced world that we live in today. Your attitude towards this all-important job is what will make it fun and exciting for both of you. My parenting understanding is deeply rooted in the belief of loving and respecting the individuality and uniqueness of every child. Children are wonderful gifts, a blessing from God.

To raise a happier, healthier, confident and responsible child, approach your parenting journey by identifying the intended outcome, and then applying the proper ingredients to achieve the desired results. It's like baking a cake with all the correct ingredients or moulding a piece of clay to a beautiful piece of pottery. As long as it is done with massive amounts of love, respect, gentleness and affection, you will have joy and success.

'Success is the progressive realisation of a worthy ideal'

Denis Waitley

Success comes from love, motivation and taking action. Always have a can-do attitude in life and your child will learn that from you. Your child will learn by what you are and what you do, rather than what you tell and teach them. Children will usually respond well when respect and cooperation are shown to them. You can replace habits that fuel conflicts with those that defuse and resolve conflict. They learn their values from you and will do what you do!

Be intuitive, compassionate, and work with your unique challenges of raising your child with perseverance, flexibility, patience, sensitivity and enjoyment.

Though raising well-adjusted children is challenging, a loving, respectful, and positive parent can make all the difference in the world. Be sure they realise how much you love them and how important it is that they are happy. This does not mean let them do whatever they want. It does mean, however, letting them know that you love them and are there for them under every possible condition.

I trust you will be able to implement most of these simple guidelines shared in this book to give you the building blocks you require to build your child who will grow to be a confident, responsible successful teen and adult. Enjoy every stage of your child's life.

Wishing you and your family vibrant health, mental clarity, and radiant well-being. May love, forgiveness, thankfulness, peace and joy abound in your life.

Enza

Enza Lyons
Licensed Brain Gym® Teacher/Consultant (Brain Gym® International/ Educational Kinesiology Foundation)
Kinesiology Practitioner (Member of A.K.A., A.T.M.S.)
Learning & Behavioural Specialist
Rhythmic Movement Training Consultant
Workplace Performance Coach

Brisbane, Australia
www.dlhc.com.au

Cherish every moment

I won't always cry, Mummy,
When you leave the room,

and my supermarket tantrums,
Will end too soon.

I won't always wake, Daddy,
For cuddles through the night
and one day you will miss,
Having a chocolate face to wipe.

You won't always wake to find my foot
Kicking you out of bed
Or find me sideways on your pillow
Where you want to lay your head
You won't always have to carry me
In a sleep from the car
Or piggy back me down the road
When my little legs can't walk
That far...

So cherish every cuddle
Remember them all-important
One day Mummy
I won't be this small

Author Unknown

 **Goals for 30 days**

Now work out what goals you want to set for your child and write them in the space below. Set your goals and be specific. Health and fitness, Family, Education, Skills and talents for income, Career, Spiritual gifts.

 **Goals for this year**

 **Goals for the next 7 years**

How old will your child be in 7 years time?

Where, what, when and how to achieve your goals.

CHAPTER 9

Finding Support

This book was written to help you understand how our children learn and of the factors that can affect their health, their learning processes, and their happiness. I trust that you have gleaned some excellent tools that you can apply to your relationship with your child, starting today!

These additional resources can be of immeasurable value as you and your child grow happily together.

Books and Resources
So where do you find that support?

There are many books and resources relating to learning, child development and the Brain Gym® program and Rhythmic Movement training. My recommendations can be found on my website at www.dlhc.com.au at Enza's Store.

Smart Moves: Why Learning Is Not All In Your Head. Carla Hannaford. Salt Lake City: Great River Books, 2005

Awakening the Child Heart. Handbook of Global Parenting. Carla Hannaford. Captain Cook: Jamilla Nur, 2002

Brain Gym®: Teachers Edition: The Companion Guide to Brain Gym®: Simple Activities for Whole-Brain Learning. Paul E. Dennison Ph.D. and Gail E. Dennison. Ventura: Edu-Kinaesthetics, 2010

Brain Gym® and Me: Reclaiming the Pleasure of Learning. Paul E. Dennison Ph.D. and Gail E. Dennison. Ventura: Edu-Kinaesthetics, 2006

Respectful Parents, Respectful Kids: 7 Keys to Turn Family Conflict Into co-operation. Sura Hart and Victoria Kindle Hodson, Puddle Dancer Press, 2006

Brain Gym®: Simple Activities for Whole Brain Learning. Paul E. Dennison Ph.D. and Gail E. Dennison. Ventura: Edu-Kinaesthetics, 2000

Movements that Heal: Rhythmic Movement Training and Primitive Reflexes Integration: a drug-free approach to learning, emotional and behavioural challenges. Harald Blomberg M.D. with Moira Dempsey, 2011

Educate Your Brain: Use Mind-Body Balance To Learn Faster, Work Smarter and Move More Easily Through Life. Kathy Brown. Balance Point Publishing, 2012

Reflexes, Learning and Behaviour: A Window into the Child's Mind. Sally Goddard. Eugene: Fern Ridge Press, 2002

Physical Activities for Improving Children's Learning and Behaviour. Billye Ann Cheatum and Allison A. Hammond Human Kinetics, 2000

The Brain That Changes Itself: Stories of Personal Triumph from the Frontiers of Brain Science. Norman Doidge. New York: Penguin, 2007

Hands On: How to Use Brain Gym® in the Classroom. Isabel Cohen and Marcelle Goldsmith. Ventura: Edu-Kinaesthetics, 2000

CD/Book: Movement & Learning: The Children's Song Book and Music CD. Brendan O'Hara. Victoria, Australia: The F# Music Company, 1991

Is your child's brain starving? Dr Michael R. Lyon MD & Dr G. Christine Laurell Ph.D.

Water: For Health, For Healing, For Life: You're Not Sick, You're Thirsty. Dr F. Batmanghelidj. M.D. New York: Riverhead, 2006

Pre-Parenting: Nurturing Your Child from Conception. Verny, T. R. and Pamela Weintraub, New York, Simon & Schuster, 2002

Magical Parent, Magical Child. Nevada City, CA, Mendizza, M. and J. C. Pearce, Touch the Future. 2001

The Biology of Belief: Unleashing the Power of Consciousness, Matter and Miracles by Bruce Lipton, Ph.D. 2005

Brain Gym® and Edu-K Courses

You may like to know even more about the Brain Gym®/ Educational Kinesiology Program. Brain Gym® is the registered trademark of Brain Gym® International/Educational Kinesiology Foundation (Brain Gym® International of Ventura, California)

To find worldwide Brain Gym® instructors and consultants –

www.braingym.org   Around the World
www.braingym.org.au   Australia
www.dlhc.com.au   Enza Lyons, Brisbane, Queensland, Australia

Rhythmic Movement Training

To find worldwide RMT Classes, teachers and consultants

www.rhythmicmovement.com

www.dlhc.com.au   Enza Lyons, Brisbane, Queensland, Australia

Brain Gym® is a registered trademark of Brain Gym® International/Educational Kinesiology Foundation.

Enza Lyons, is a licensed Brain Gym® instructor/consultant, kinesiology practitioner, learning & behavioural specialist, rhythmic movement training consultant and author. She has been involved with Brain Gym® since 1986. For over 23 years in her private practice, she has assisted children and adults struggling with concentration, memory, comprehension, reading, writing, math, anxiety, depression, trauma, pain, early learning difficulties such as ADD, ADHD, dyspraxia, dyslexia, autism and delayed development. Clearly one can see these children are intelligent, just stuck.

She has transformed lives with outstanding results using effective and non-conventional educational learning programs. These programs can unlock your child's hidden talents to learn, create, move and achieve success at school and in life.

Young parents can be better informed to assist them in making better choices to help their children build confidence, self-esteem, increase their ability to learn and relate better to others. Enza shares her passion and enthusiasm with others through courses, workshops, in-house school training, conference presentations and her private sessions. She teaches Brain Gym® in the Classroom, Brain Gym® for the Workplace, Brain Gym® for over 50's, Brain Gym® 101, Optimal Brain Organisation, Vision Circles and Rhythmic Movement Training workshops.

For more information contact Enza Lyons, Brisbane, Australia on *www.dlhc.com.au.* Enza travels around Australia teaching workshops and provides personal consultations.

Bonus Offer

Join Enza's membership program to learn techniques and exercises to help your child succeed. Parents can benefit too! Join the **Dynamic Learning Program** now and get the **First Month FREE.**

Go to **www.dlhc.com.au/enza-lyons-services/dynamic-learning-program** to **receive your Special gifts with Bonuses for you to keep** when you join. Enjoy!

Learn more about her products and services at www.dlhc.com.au

Printed in Australia
AUOC02n1348070414
260550AU00006B/6/P

9 780987 341525